THE POETS SYMPHONY

VERSES, MELODIES & LYRICAL POEMS

THE POETS SYMPHONY

VERSES, MELODIES & LYRICAL POEMS

edited by tara caribou

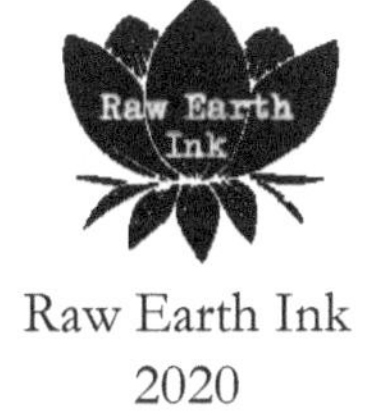

Raw Earth Ink
2020

This book is a work of poetry and art.

First paperback edition May 2020

Book design and editing by tara caribou

Cover design by bookcoverzone.com

ISBN 978-1-7330808-5-9 (paperback)

Published by Raw Earth Ink
PO Box 39332
Ninilchik, Alaska USA 99639
www.taracaribou.com

Table of Contents

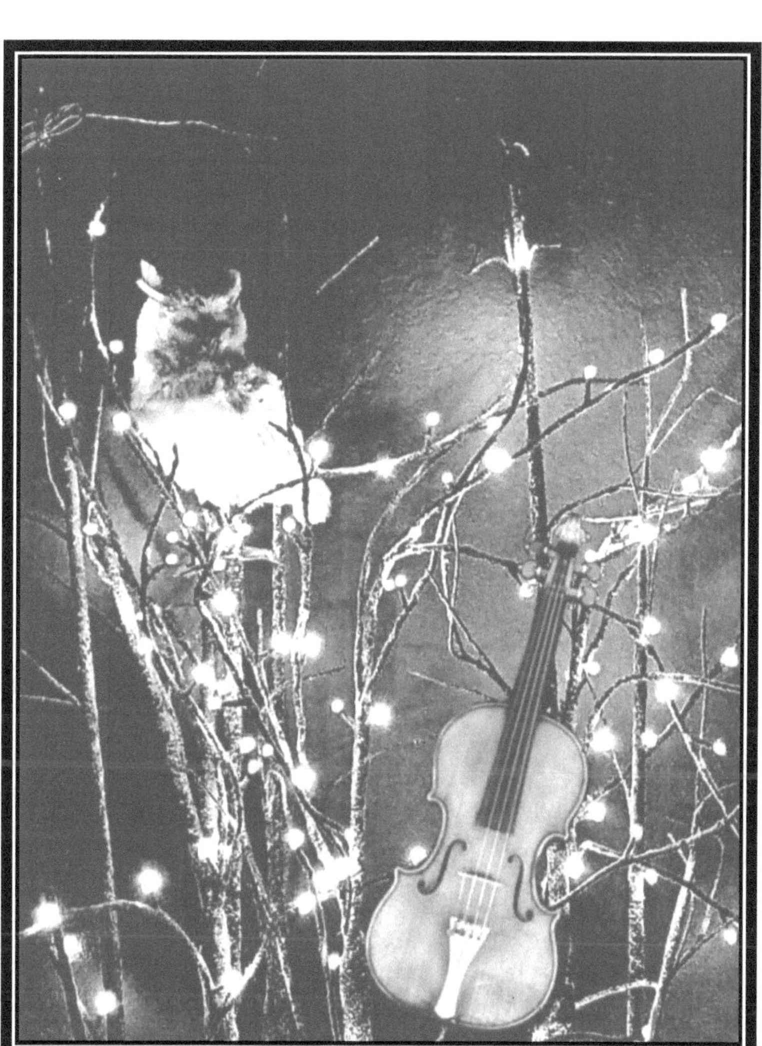

"Viola's Muse"

ValentinA Saldaña

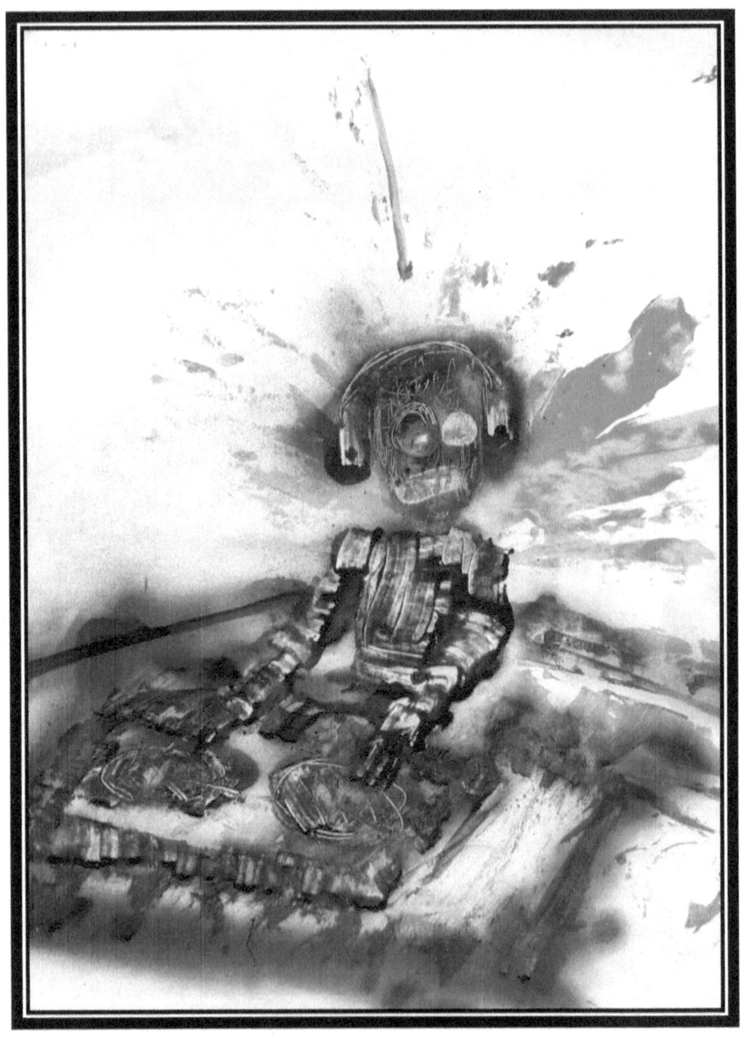

"He's the DJ, I'm the Rapper

Ody West

Overture

Delicately the conductor lifted his hands.
We paused in anticipation, on the edge of our seats.
The calm, the silence, pregnant and full.
Swiftly dropping them once more, the music began.

THE IVORY BATON

by CG Tenpenny

Tap, tap, tap.

"Let it begin,"

said the conductor,
as he tapped his
baton again.
White, like ivory,
it rapped
the music stand,
leaving a dent
for each beat spent on
the mournful timpani.

The shadow symphony
screamed in the dark,

"Bedlam! Cacophony!"

As the conductor smiled
his manic grin,
chaos erupted from the reeds
and winds.

The apex, pinnacle, and peak,
was reached by each player,
out of time, out of key,
but the fevered conductor
tapped his baton
through the rise and fall
of his masterpiece...

Anxiety.

SURFING STATION TO STATION

by J Matthew Waters

I turn the dial to 107.9 fm
but all I hear is ozzie or zepplin
van halen or ac/dc

I tell myself if I want to hear classic rock
I'd dial in 100.3 or maybe 105.7

whatever happened to my once
favorite retreat called rock 108
where I could always hear
something beautifully brand new
no matter how good or bad

I mean seriously
is there really not enough new rock
to make the world go 'round anymore

the population on this planet
continues to explode
but meanwhile
I'm stuck here half-dazed
(from all the static)
surfing station to station
hoping to find a brand-new groove

LONGEVITY

by Piano Girl

Picture me, almost seven
Stringy hair in my eyes
Sitting at the piano
As Grandma smiles
Hands on keys, eyes on notes
Melodies flowing clear
Sharing music from my heart
Though young in years

Picture me, fifty-two
Working to hide the gray
Teaching music to little ones
Exhausted every day
Hands on keys, eyes on notes
Melodies flowing clear
Sharing music from my heart
Now in middle-age

Picture me, ninety-nine
Grey hair in a bun
Glasses perched on the end of my nose
Ready for some fun
Hands on keys, eyes on notes
Melodies flowing clear
Sharing music from my heart
After all these years

TIME SIGNATURE

by Hidden Bear

Everyone get in line
Now count 1,2,3,4,5
That's right 5/4 time
Familiar but a little odd
Hard to have your head nod

A Signature!
A Time Signature!
A Odd-Meter Time Signature!

No backbeat to tap your feet
It's comfortable after 4 but no more
See as the 5 note hits its splits
Your attention strained hard to maintain
Or describe to someone this odd one

Beat unkept, sloppy, and weird
Like a kiss against a rough beard
Its beat is random and off tempo
Like my heartbeat when you get too close
I guess I'll two step and waltz
Until I escape your love's vault
So I'll get myself in line
And count 1,2,3,4,5

TANGLED-UP IN RHYMES

by Mark Tulin

Dylan came to call,
singing a sardonic tune, playing
a mouth harp, moaning sweet words
that descended from a melancholy sky.

I was ready for the man who launched
a hundred marches that invoked
a thousand verses of wisdom, twisted
and tangled-up in rhymes.

He came down from the mount
with his irreverent twang,
old acoustic tunes
that he once sang in heaven
before he was born again.

Between soulful moments,
he sipped water to wet his aged throat,
stretching his legs under the piano,
wiping his sweaty brow of musical eternity.

RHYTHM

by Hidden Bear

I wish I could play the drums
Sticks in my hand; blisters on my thumbs
That convoluted mechanism of rhythm
Making combinations as light from a prism
Hearing the tick of a closed high-hat keeping time
While I splash in snare and bass drum to find
That familiar back beat
That supports everyone from Coltrane to Backstreet
The sounds underneath every track
That makes your head nod and feet tap
Holding down the pace of each tune
Guiding guitar, singer, violin, and bassoon

With this skill I could travel as a rock star
Sunglasses, tank tops looking cool as my drums rock hard
Adding drama with my talented fills
Creating a cacophony as crowds thrill
Yes, if I could play the drums I'd join a cover band
Play weddings about walking hand in hand
Getting everyone to dance to Mumbo No. 5
All the kids air drumming as dancers traipse by

But I can't play the drums I just have the rhythm
I put down the sticks and my dreams with them
I'm confined to the beats of my words
Though the fans don't come in herds
My tempo is my own
Poetry, not drums, my home.

VOODOO KING

by Braeden Michaels

Like a stick of vicious dynamite
A character decorated with flash
Articulate and animated multiplied by ten
Personality dipped in precision
Nicknamed "Excellence of Supremacy"
Drifting into his white magic and black charm
Coliseum shakes, thousands thrash
A tongue laced with power and delight
Platinum albums counted on each finger
Vocals spiked with fury and wildfire
Serenading ghost, breathtaking quill
Blister deepens on his left cheek
Drifting into his white magic and black charm
Amphitheater rattles, thousands in unison
Ink slinger born in God's smoke and water
An iron originator, wicked scribbler
Intensity engraved within his veins
Bearing scars like a torch in the night
Eyes colored of amber and brick
Drifting into his white magic and black charm
Stadium erupted, thousands applaud
Complexion soaked from waterfalls of grace
Vivid from a translucent point of view
Ambrosial concoction of sounds
Blending miracles, vexation, and authenticity
Colliding jackhammer riffs and stonewashed chords
Drifting into his white magic and black charm
Arena pulsates, thousands sing in harmony

THE RESCUE

by Piano Girl

Eyes follow notes
Notes become phrases
Phrases grow into melodies
Fingers to keys
Keys to hammers
Hammers to strings
Familiar sounds
Escape the piano
Filling the room
Calming anxious thoughts
Rescuing me
From the waves

FIRST MEETING

by Gary Bradshaw

Over a rapid 'drum-roll' bass,
the first subject
erupts
as though escaping
from great tension.

The second subject,
which travels rapidly
between bass and treble,
sustains the mood of
nervous intensity.
This is reinforced at the end
of the exposition
by recalling the
first subject
in the key of the
second.

The solidity of the
Introduction
returns before the development
darts away
playing with fragments
of the link passage between
first and second subjects
and the
introduction's
passionate melody.

SYMPHONY

by A. P. Christopher

There, as if drawn by the orchestral notes of despair
Where strings are the echoes of confidence never reclaimed
Violins strung with the promise of pain in the air
And played with a bow that could never be tamed
For eternity built it with only a strand of your hair

I, as the listener, lingered where longing provoked
The somber refrain of the melody best never heard
Cellos were playing the darkest and deepest of notes
A cadence of crying that carefully lured
Me to temples, where tired and tearful, I tragically spoke

There, in the chamber, were tapestries painted of you
And organs were weeping the hymns of your final farewell
Timpanis were pulsing - the beat of my heart as you flew
And left on my lips were the words in a swell
A crescendo intended, now suddenly hollow and few

I, as the watcher, was singing the last of my songs
Where notes are the humming of rain in the days that I wait
Trumpets of tragedy, mournfully playing along
And all that I have are the words I create
In a symphony where you were music - and words don't belong

YOUNGER ME

by Piano Girl

If I could talk to
The younger me
So many things
I would say
Slow down
There is no hurry
To grow up
Time simply passes
Hours at the piano
Will not be in vain
They serve to
Ease your mind
Scars that form
On the inside
Remain hidden
Unless shared
Don't be afraid
To express them
Through music
Through words
Mistakes?
Do not define
Yet, admission
Offers healing, help
Choices
Good and bad
Play a role in
Who you become
Perhaps those words
Would help her know
The future is bright
She will be okay

PLAY IT FUCKING LOUD!

(Dylan, Manchester Free Trade Hall, 1966)

by S J Reizlein

Judas! a shout from the audience,
Bob's dismissive reply,
You are liar, I don't believe you,
As he turns to The Band
Play it fucking loud! the order,
So it starts, electric thrill,
Like a Rolling Stone

Dylan's on fire, and The Band plays loud,
Train whistle hoots, words elongate,
Stooone, ooown, hooome,
Lines finish in nasal howl-ends, trail across
Great lakes and prairies to dull north England,
Mid-May nights, mid-sixties cool, his hot jet
Telecaster, new Chelsea boots skip and twirl,
Megaphone hands, cupped mouth spits out
the words, can't look back, this is the future.

HARMONY

by Hidden Bear

Melody is great that I can't deny
Carrying songs like birds as they fly
She defines the line that the music makes
Making legends out of singers who have what it takes
Stealing the stage from every distracting fill
Making out ears bend to her will

However my true love is her sister Harmony
Always in the background not far from me
She is shy at times and keeps silent
But when her voice sings its vibrant
Adding complexity and power
To Melody's vocal hour

Yes, the shy sister in the back calling clearly
The notes changed slightly ring beautifully
Each a little higher or lower based on Melody's mood
Yes, without melody there's no harmony or tune
But Harmony is the dark horse racing steadily
Chasing right on the heels of melody
Harmony has more talent and everyone knows
Melody is the easy rhythm to Harmony's subtle prose
Behind melody's shining spotlight
Is Harmony's backlit highlight

Harmony wants to shine like Melody
But too loud she'll create disunity
She always plays the backstage, out of sight
Behind melody, holding notes close but not too tight

MYSTERY

by Piano Girl

An array of dots
Linked together
Symbolic sentences
Filling a grid
Five lines
Four spaces
A curious
Work of art
Waiting–for
Eyes to read
Hands to play
Ears to hear
Sounds escape
Rising and falling
Filling the silence
Listen and discover
A beautiful mystery
Melody

CLOSE THE LID

by CG Tenpenny

Close the lid,
I can play nothing else.

A yellow rose rests on the music shelf.

When the rose was fresh,
I fumbled on the keys.

The middle C,

the compromise,
was truly out of reach,
because the left hand
insisted on its selfish beat.

Out of key, and
black and white it seems,
this song for the Rose
intoned sadness,
reminding me
of the missing pages
I could not see.

The yellow rose was dead and dried.

Like an old parchment,
tucked in my songbook,
the yellow rose became the
missing pages,
and finally, I understood
the signature and time…

but, it's a minor thing.

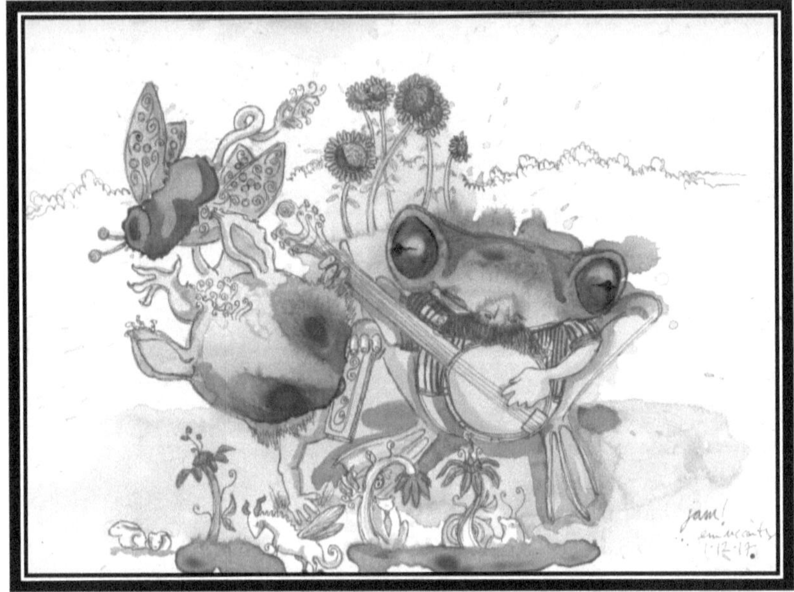

"Jam!"

emje mccarty

Crescendo

His hands forged magic before our glistening eyes.
Visions of love and nature growing, we faded.
The dance of bows and fingers a shadow,
Replaced by the burgeoning story he wove.

CHOIR OF THE TREES

by Robert Birkhofer

Have you, my dear friend, heard
The choir of the trees?
The songs they sing when roused
By playful, pleasant breeze?
Have you, my dear friend, heard
The stories the trees tell?
The secrets that they sing
To those who listen well?
Now, wise man I am not
A fool I may well be
But I have found some peace
By list'ning to the trees
I heard sweet, soft pine leaves
Whisp'ring andante chords
Forming a melody
Upon the earth to pour
Wolves joined in the refrain
The rivers swelled as well
And all creation formed
A joyous ensemble
The choir sang as one
Their voices rose until
The great crescendo peaked
Bidden by nature's will
A wond'rous sound it was
Much joy from it I gained
Long after the last note
Its memory remained
So, next time that you hear
The trees singing their song
I hope you'll stop awhile
Perhaps ev'n sing along
They'll share music with you
And share their wisdom too
And blessed to hear you'll be
The choir of the trees

THE CALL

by M Ennenbach

she sat upon the rocks
ignoring
the spray of saltwater
as it burst
over her head
her eyes shut
as she sang
in an ethereal voice
that carried
cross the waves
to find my ear
a delicate undercut
to the storms
raging
around me
I sailed
away from home
from all I knew
in search
of an end
to bad beginnings
the moment I heard
her call
I felt myself
stand at the railing
all I wanted
was to answer
as I dove into the choppy water
her song pulling me
against exhaustion
against the voice
screaming
this was doomed
to fail
as I swam
I caught a glimpse
of her naked frame
in the ocean spray
her song filled me
with light
as the water

filled my lungs
as I sank
into the deep
my last image
was her ravenous smile
rows of sharp fangs
and her song
mocking
as I died

SURROUND SOUND ELEMENTS

by ValentinA Saldaña

stones so serene and yet
their composition pulsates
she is a rock christened "The Royal 8"
synthesized layers of the harmonic crystal
an ornament of high vibration
an arrangement of eight minerals
holy instruments in a band
like no other on earth

water water in everything everywhere
drown in its mild manic medleys
splashed against a face it awakens
hear it pour as it fills a cup
drops fall from the sky
beat on skin like drums
slide into a tub at the end of each day
the warm rhythm of fluid soothes speaks

wind symphonies swirl
breeze tickles the chimes
outside of sanctuaries
leaves rustle off of branches
blow blow blow away
so sweet so soft their ballet

fire burns crackles
crispy notes dance in flames
upwards towards the sky
subtle smoke whispers
a spicy incense silence

spiritual space
an intricately humble
background
ever-present everlasting
an a capella song
sung by a kindred choir
inside of a chapel

A LIGHT AT THE OPERA

by Shane Windham

She used to let me watch our future
play out, one ballad at a time
In the soundtrack of my life,
she's all I ever leave on repeat

I remember not seeing my favorite band
play my favorite number
because she wanted to make love
in the parking lot instead
And, the truth is that I think
it was everyone in the stadium
who missed the superior show
To hear them while feeling her;
there really are no words for describing it

I clearly recall the shimmering clang
of her bedroom mix echoing off the walls
in that lonely, indoor pool we used to frequent
for a far sight more than night-swimming
She kept the volume so loud
that we could make out the vocals
with our heads under water
Our bodies would sway in slow motion
as one beneath the surface,
in spite of that sharp increase
in the speed of those splashes
dancing around us

She used to play my recordings
as she played with herself;
I once got to watch with a guitar in hand
We were an unforgettable spin,
to say the very least,
but only the best records know when to end
And, who among us is bold enough to say
that there's no room for she and I
in another crowded theater;
in yet another Top 100?

Maybe someday we'll give
love's stereo another go

LOVE (IN B MINOR)

by Mark Ryan

Call me when the sound reaches your ear.
Let me know when the heavens fall to earth.
It came on hurried wings to my soul.
Trapped in amber and lodge in my heart.
Heralded by the holy who stand guard.
Watching my world for fear of falling.
A tuneful bliss submerges this decay.
Spilling into my soul like water and manna.
A heady mix of the forbidden and the deserved.
I hear you in every conversation.
The pitched key of life plays you out.
Your mouth seals for nothing but kisses.
Trumpeting in explosions as you breathe into me.
Love, in b-minor.
A scaled resonance of lust and locomotion.
A majored ambience that now sets in my heart.
Like a pip to a fruit.
Taste me sweetly, and spit out the seeds of sorrow.
These sounds suffocate.
Penetrate.
And masturbate through to another form.
A selfless knowing of one.
In the arms of no other, but a shrouded thing of beauty.
Lying on the keys of my heart.

CELLO

by Cassa Bassa

Crooked spikes of the rustic iron gate licking the hellfire sky
Luring sound of the cello playing softly to whisper promise of happy memories and haunting stories
His footsteps on the garden path pebbles are giving away kernels of excitement
Restraint by the French windows, he swallows at the view of her untarnished body wrapping around the maple cello
She exhibits as the most porcelain icy celestial body on the Kuiper belt
The divine tone of cello is escalating from mellow to vibrant, lustrous to transcendental to dark
The forbidden pleasure shoots through his legs, groin, abdomen to his heart forming a lump in his Adam's apple
He dares not let out the primal cry, not even a low groan to disturb the masterful performance
The vibration slapping his core in ebbs and flows
His rhythmic breathing orchestrates harmoniously with the evocative cello melody to reach the pinnacle of perfection
When the silence finally falls and the music gives in to exhaustion, their eyes meet, locked in a fulfilling gaze

OCTOBER'S ORCHESTRA

by ValentinA Saldaña

i headed to the cemetery
to share with you my rose
the sun was bright and beautiful
how warm October's glow
i paused to visit angels
around the autumn pond
the willow trees wept
as they sang our song
i of course beckoned
by humming along
the pansies danced
around my feet
they know what lies
beneath
oak leaves played
within the wind
a symphony so sweet
i buried letters in the earth
i sent them with my heart
then i laid on top of them
willed the ground to part
all i heard were starlings
flying round and round
i pray they keep my secrets
until the day i'm found

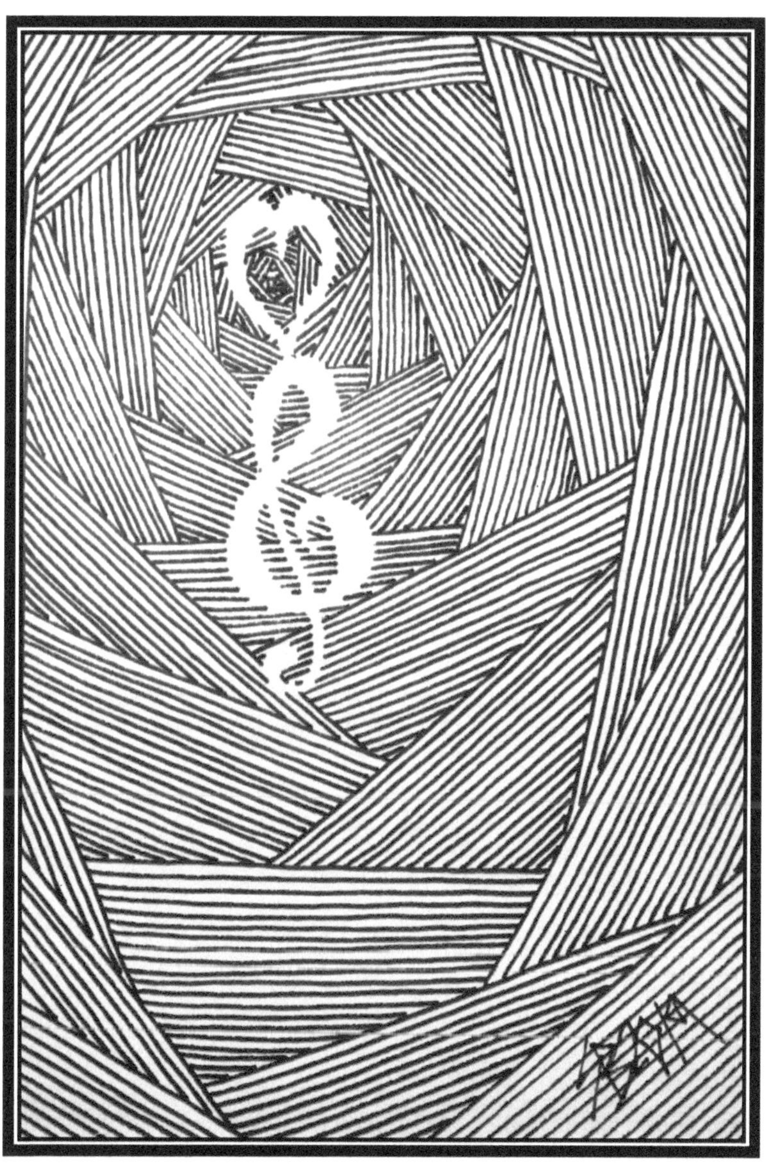

"If Music Be the Food of Love…"

Steven Bryson

I SEE RED

by Mark Ryan

My eyes itch and my heart heaves.
Reading over and over.
Line after line.
A melody of time.
Pulling me out of traffic, pulling me into your frame.
Surround yourself with good intentions.
A swirling world of your black and white.
Yet all I see is red.
The swan song that you misunderstand.
Plucking my heartstrings for the correct rhythm.
The right sound.
Color your lines. Careful now, make it pretty.
This is the page we're on, this is the hymn we'll sing.
Notes to take note of.
My story snipped down to a sentence.
The finches' song bottled in a jar.
A sentence that mice can devour.
In your book of course, to your own tune.
What was I thinking?

SAVE

by Candice Louisa Daquin

I'm the girl who wants to go out dressed in sequins
dance under a velvet ball bathed in violet light
drink silver wine and slither to pulsing music

I'm the girl who wants to stay in a cave dressed in leaves
wash my hair in a cold stream and forget to speak
sleep with silent moons under my hair

I'm too many things and not enough
I'm everything and I'm nothing
I'm tired and I can't sleep
I'm exhausted of life and I've only just begun
I cry at everything and I feel nothing
I dream of nightmares and in my nightmares have dreams
I'm where the wild things are
and I'm okay
at being everything and nothing.

VIBRATOS OF OUR LOVE

by Jamila Wardak

Our love consists of vibratos
I want the world to hear, someday
For now I sing it silently to myself
The shower, my current stage

I've rehearsed so many times
I've memorized every note
One day I wish the world can hear
The beautiful story we wrote

For now I will cherish our secret
Savor every line
My love for you will continue to grow
And get louder throughout time

It sounds like I'm eager
It's such a beautiful tune
I want the world to hear it
But it could wear out too soon

We shall continue to sing in secret
Until wedding bells chime
Then our song of love will play
But I will be whispering every line

Our love consists of vibratos
I love and cherish so much
I want the world to sing it with me
My world, just you and I

MUSE

by A.P. Christopher

An easy laugh and smile
And a radiance that spreads a mile
Wrapped within an aura
Cast in shades too deep to reconcile

Set within such simple words
What should be level nouns and verbs
Are cadences of symphonies
Of harps and strings and timpani

Azure eyes like calm lagoons
Surrounding coals, like island blooms
A veritable Crete
A siren song that sings a subtle tune

Beneath, a spark spontaneous
That burns and glows in gradients
A candlelight in gloom
A cast of stars against a fading moon

ME, YOU, AND JOEY RAMONE AT THE END OF THE WORLD

by M Ennenbach

it is a simple chord progression
churning in the inner ear
as we share headphones
watching the sun set
over the ocean
hey ho, let's go! hey ho, let's go!
i watch as you
mouth the words
toes tapping
the autumn leaves
as the pinkish purple bruise
spreads across the water before us
they're forming on a straight line
above the missiles soar
streaking across the sky
leaving white trailed love letters
to spontaneous combustion
as they fly towards the city
they're all revved up and ready to go
your eyes on mine
the impending doom
an afterthought
in the moment of pure
subsonic bliss
playing between beats of our heart
pulsating to the backbeat
a rumble
shakes the ground
as the bass
rattles our inner ears
the sun in front of us
as pure white light shines behind
the kids are losing their minds
me and you and joey ramone
waiting
for the shockwave to hit
as the world burns down
around us

TICKLING THE IVORIES

by Mark Ryan

Cotton madness wraps around my soul.
You take me in, and strip me bare.
Pedal push the valve in my heart.
Which pumps to a beat unheard in dreams.
For that is where I must be.
Swimming in the clouded state of sleep.
You lick the touch of a fingertip punch.
On skin that stretches and aches.
My ivory tower tumbles into sheets.
And you play my spine each vertebrae at a time.
Tickling the ribs like un-played ivory keys.
Your fingers tiptoeing in tune.
The sound you hear is happiness.
It drifts and bellows all at once.
All for an audience of two.
Until the sound of silence takes hold.
Gripping with the same intensity that lays upon me.
For I hold this breath that you dangerously covert.
Stealing in a second with your well-versed hand.
So nimble those bones are played.
And all air is lost to a dream, one I give in to.
Exhaled and invisible like the sound of love.

UNCHAINED MELODY

by Leon Jones

You're a work of instrumental genius,
Aesthetically breathtaking,
I was mesmerized by your first tune,
ecstatically, I'm tuned to your calibration.
You have Serenaded my soul,
I'm so soothed and in awe of your orchestration!
For your ethereal sound is a heavenly symphony.
Bathed in transcendent passion,
I have found in you affinity.
Your angelic melodious resonance,
moves my soul like a calm breeze,
for at ease is my heart,
you know the right pitch to play,
blissful notes on my heart strings.
in sync with your rhythm,
you know my cadence,
we lockstep to the same rhythm,
truly you're the song to my heart
that's perfectly written.

SENSATION'S COMPILATION

by Shane Windham

The alcohol in my blood
is a guitar solo
Your body is
the curvature of the Cosmos
I'd gladly pay the price
of an instant death
just to know every sound
you're capable of making
You bid me to press upon you
some random combination
You reward me
with a pleasurable melody
My movements imitate your aria,
and I'm asked to pretend
that we're equals in evocation
But, you're immediate obsession
You're one unforgettable transition
after another
How long have I been swimming
in the din of your scented feel?
How will life beyond
this handful of moments
ever come close
to meaning as much?
Connected at both ends
of this collective vibration,
we can but sense the reverberating
reality of perfection
pulsing its way out of existence;
complacent warmth, lulling us
toward the company
of lesser dreams
But, should I find you there, anew,
let us sing a second refrain

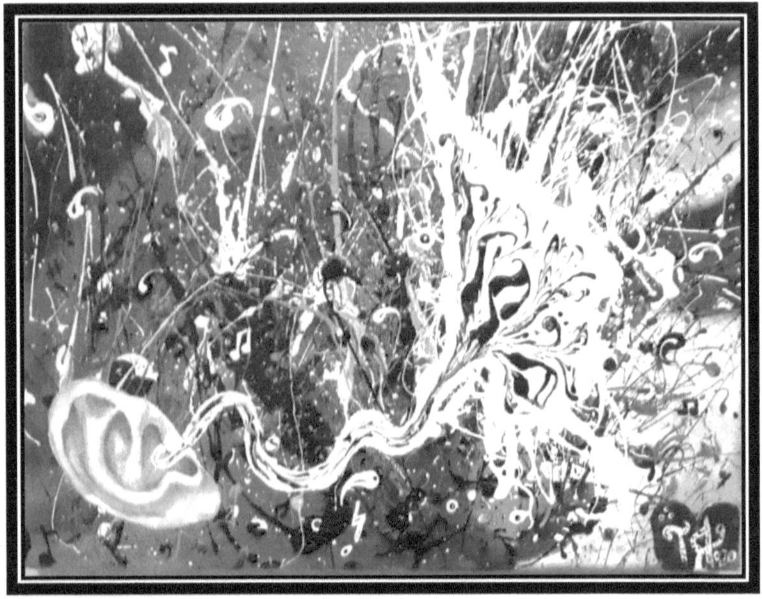

"Symphonic Climax"

TJ

Ostinato

Again and again we felt the push and the pull.
Lyrics and rhymes rose in our minds unbidden.
Drums echoed woodwinds, the brass reverberated.
The notes and sounds reproducing his movements.

THE SYMPHONY'S GHOST

by Braeden Michaels

Between the fascination and the bloom
a cello vibrates within her devotion
Between the radiance and the exhilaration
a piano plays with her intellect

The symphony plays for her imperfections

Between the glitter and the rich glow
a saxophone harmonizes with her smile
Between the elegance and the charm
a violin gravitates to her spirit

The symphony plays for her wounds

Between the glamour and the splendor
a harp shimmers within her strength
Between the glare and the sunshine
a harmonica chants beside her charisma

The symphony plays for her blisters

Between the artistry and magnetism
a guitar plays inside her untouchable fire
Between her magical appeal and grace
a trombone croons in her lost sky

The symphony plays for her burnt rainbows

LIFE BEGINS WITH SOUND

by RedCat

Life begins with sound
Staccato tapping heart
Water echoes all around
Fortissimo live-spark start

Mother sets the tune
Mindset weaving loom
Building live score rune
Heartbeat, boom, boom, boom

Then the primal screams
Birthing duet score
Melody for future dreams
Sheet music lore

Round and round we go
Adagio, Allegro, Fortissimo
Learning scale and bow
Da Capo, Dal Segno, Pianissimo

Notes on the every bar
Minor, major, sharp
Melody for solo star
Bard-song and harp

Opus beat in time
As soul-light shine
Life concerto in rhyme
Diminuendo, Ritardando, Fine

EYES OF THE STORM

by Jesse Lee Staggs

Look into the eyes of the storm
Portals into pain, the norm
See the dead in the calm
Read the sorrow of the psalm
Skip ahead by twenty-two
Years gone by with nothing new
Only a better mask to wear
So, come inside if you dare

Listen to the tone of this song
Hear the hoping for hope all along
The child's cries in the dark
A melody of love left stark
I wonder if you can relate
With your heart as hard as slate
I wonder if you truly care
So, sing along if you're there

Feel the hollow echo of my heart
Bleeding for you is a form of art
The things I do just to feel alive
As I hasten towards an end I strive
To call out for help but silently
Praying for death even violently
I gave it my all and I tried my best
Just give me my end I want to rest

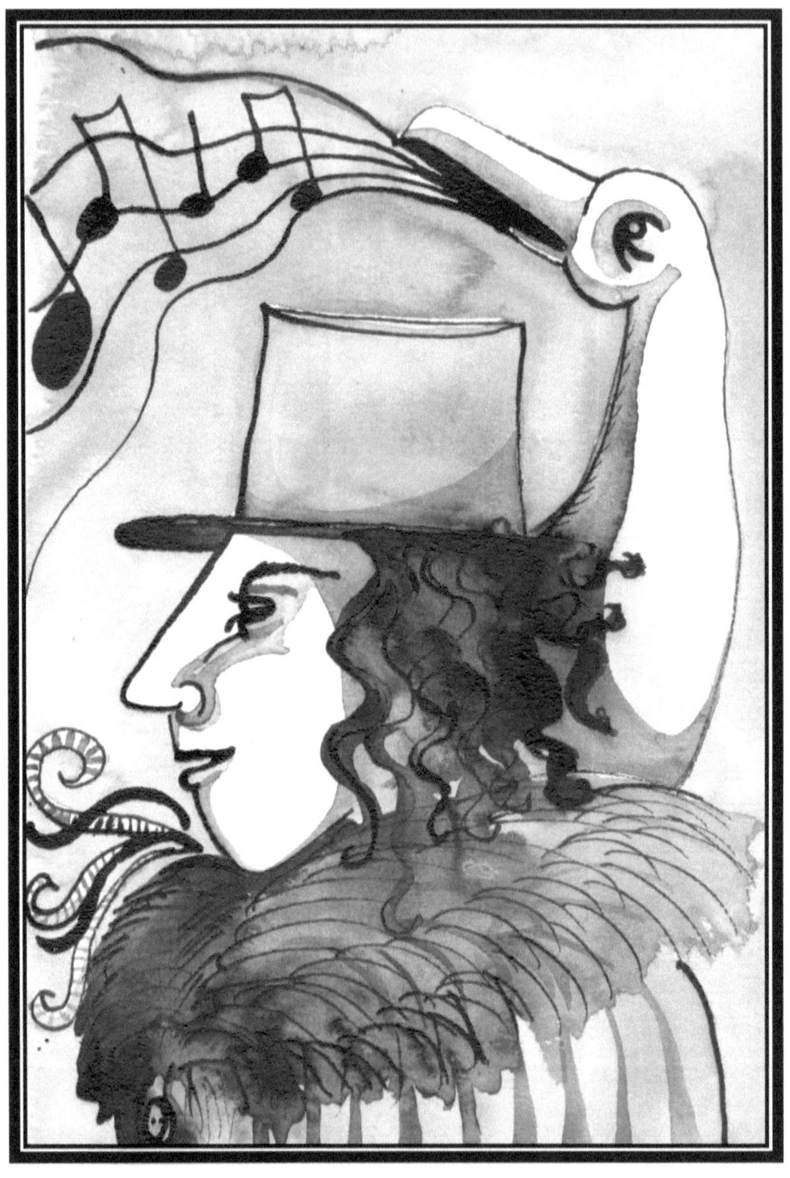

"my old friend"

emje mccarty

MUSIC WITHIN US

by Chris Nelson

It swirls around our tiny forms
This pulse, this beat, from mother's heart,
Before our ears can note the sound
The purest rhythm, sacred art.
A private ocean sings to us
A melody through every pore,
We dance to rhythms in our souls
As flexing fingers write the score.
And as into the light we go
With eyes that see and ears that hear,
We move to beats that aren't our own
But in our hearts the truth we hear.
Our voices raised we sing so loud
A chorus that defines our lives,
The words that mean so much to us
The major lifts, the minor dives.
And when the sun begins to set
And only scattered notes remain,
We feel the pulse within our hearts
And know that we are all the same;
Moving to the music
That lives within us all.

DEATH ON LUNAR WINGS

by Mark Ryan

Weak, the weary watches on.
Another time, another song.
That plays like gold inside their hearts.
And burgeons tears to fall like stars.
But when the music finally dies.
There'll be but darkness in those eyes.
A solitary symphony for the lone.
Of crownless kings with empty thrones.
For when the weary finally sleep.
It's in plastic coffins, for space to keep.

TINSEL TOWN

by Candice Louisa Daquin

Her skin is as white as her eyes are black
she steals your sins and spits them into glass
where darkness and light cavort to the sound
of splintered moments crushed and ground
your feet bleed dancing on shells
exposing diamonds and rubies and little umbilicals
strung like harpsicords around your buttered loins
where the Goathead grinds his coarse phallus
into the flesh of your yet torn pride...

Does it hurt when he fucks you straight up?
like a whiskey poured without a cup?
does it hurt when he daggers his thrust?
calls you his whore, his baby, his little puss puss?
does it hurt when they paint you in gold lame and sin?
downing your abortions with vodka and gin?
does it hurt when night becomes day and all of a sudden
the record scratches that place
where voices cannot reach and music reveals
a memory of holding the afterbirth until it congealed
still hungry for supper.

EVERYTHING CHANGES

by emje mccarty

today is the day
everything
changes
my mantra goes
from personal
to universal
everything changes
how do you shape
the change
in your life
in your soul
how do you spread change
not like a virus
but like a song
we whisper
then
we sing
today
is
the
day
everything
everything
changes
because we no longer
accept
no longer
allow
it to stay
the same

MUSIC

by A. P. Christopher

There comes a time
When all the rhymes
I have are inefficient

A forest made of paper words
A home I've made of playing cards
The songs from origami birds
They do not carry far

There comes a time
When all the lines
They amplify the difference

A world of little plastic parts
An audience of figurines
The rhythm of a porcelain heart
It knows not how to sing

There comes a time
When, "No, I'm fine..."
Just hides a flawed existence

A life made out of what-could-be's
A soul that prays to "maybe soon"
The music of a symphony
That's never quite in tune

GRACIE ANNE AND HER ONE-MAN BAND

by Mark Ryan

Gracie Ann and her one-man band.
Played each day at the village bandstand.
She played in the wind, and the sun and the rain.
She played long after she had become quite a pain.
But play on she must for its all Gracie had.
As her dreams turned to dust and her heart became sad.
The pain took its toll on poor Gracie's bones.
Playing all day to hearts turned to stone.
For though some smiled as they passed Gracie by.
Others would long for her swift last goodbye.
They looked on in disgust to her state and her frame.
Ravaged by life and its sad sea of pain.
Her hands became sore in the ice and the chill.
And numbed to the world, but she carried on still.
For she had no home to go back to at night.
No lover or friend did she have in her sight.
And inside her bones a cancer had sped.
An unknown evil that she had yet to dread.
For life had crumbled and been turned around.
The circus had stayed and she became the clown.
She played on at the bandstand through stares and disgust.
And smiled like an idiot with hope and distrust.
Hoping for a few sad bits of loose change.
Would rattle her tin in a hopeless reframe.
Till one day no tune came from her one-man band.
Indeed this woman had at last turned to sand.
And faded away into the sea like the tide.
A part of their world they still wanted to hide.
And they sold her instruments and cremated her bones.
Her soul now silent, her heart without tone.
Now when they pass the bandstand and hear nothing at all.
They do not think of Gracie Ann or her sad tragic fall.
They ignore her memory or that fact that she's dead.
And frown at the homeless that remain up ahead.

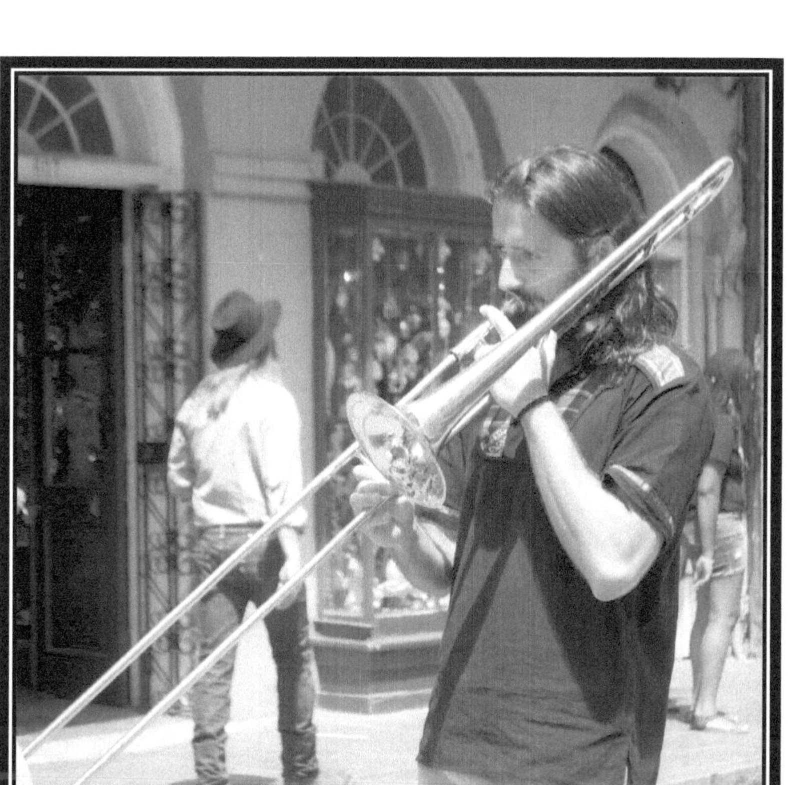

"Slide Trombone"

Easter Parade, New Orleans

Photograph: Janet Sawatsky

WOKE UP THIS MORNING

by RedCat

Woke up this morning
Beds are burning
Human behavior
Ashes of the modern world
Turning

In the air tonight
Chains of misery
Moonlight shadow
All we want is love
Carefree

Shadow on the wall
Sign your name
Primal scream
Golden age of capitalism
Overcame

Sadness hides the Sun
Change the World
Rebel Rebel
New World in the morning
Twirled

Children of the revolution
Winds of change
Nature calling
This could be the last time
Strange

THE SYMPHONY DIVINE

by Amittras Pal

I was the voyeur, in that moment all yours,
As your fingers played, the song that cures,
A moment incredible, as bow kissed the bridge,
And tunes flared, like fire on a pepperidge.

The spruce fiddle swayed, cradled in your arm,
I watched powerless, seduced by your charm.
You opened your eyes, and saw me watching you,
Up-tempo'ed with a smile, 'was that a cue?'

Like lovers hold hands, when they walk along,
Metronome partnered truly, your lovely song.
Your radiant eyes gazed, into those of mine,
Seemed to beckon me close, like a pull divine.

I inched closer, perhaps a little too quick!
Slowed me down alright, a sharp tonal flick.
Then your smile, and the slowed bow assented,
From voyeur to an actor, I was now ascended.

Your nod pointed me, to another laid aside,
I picked the violin, ready to join your ride,
Our notes made love, like a symphony divine,
At crescendo we said, "Will you be mine?"

TEARDROPS OF THE SUNSET

by Braeden Michaels

I've sat beside my teardrops of the sunset
to watch my soul bleed into the river

I've sat among my teardrops of the sunset
and wrote poetry to the echoes of the morning

I've sat close to my teardrops of the sunset
and lyrics from the inside lash out

I've sat side by side with my teardrops of the sunset
to breathe in the sky

I've sat adjacent to my teardrops of the sunset
to gasp at the beauty of the rain

I've sat near my teardrops of the sunset
to observe silence was the beginning to the end

TURN UP THE MUSIC

by emje mccarty

despair sends me
postcards
but i don't go to my mailbox
depression
rings me
on the phone
but i don't answer
rage knocks
at the door
i just turn up the music
and dance…
this is today
tomorrow is anyone's
guess
will darkness consume me
will magic
music
and art
keep me safe
keep me sane?
in the end
all i have
is today
today
i just turn up the music
and dance

DANCE ME TO MY DEATH
(FOR ANDREA)

by ValentinA Saldaña

Dance me to my death
Only I can hear the song
I don't like to dance alone
It just feels so wrong

Life was so unkind
Solitary for so long
Mirrors remind me
I will soon be gone

I did not comprehend
What she tried not to say
As she laid on her bed
What became our final day

My heart yearns a return
To the place we first met
I promise to linger longer
To be present no regret

She did not hear my voice
She did not see my face
She did not feel my heart
She missed my embrace

I will ask her to forgive
The ways I did not show
How much I adored her
I will never let her go

Dance me to my death
Only I can hear the song
I don't like to dance alone
It just seems so wrong

TO HEAR YOUR SONG

by Chris Nelson

It's oh so very late
The city falls asleep
I left them at the gate
The songs that make me weep.
I'm oh so very tired
I've counted every sheep
I wanted to feel wired
Wanted to take the leap.

It's oh so very still
Without your melody
The sounds that always fill
The hole that grows in me.
A song that lives between
The sheets that hold our lives
The lyrics never seen
A melody of life.

And I will play you like a harp,
Strum my fingers through your soul,
Pluck the strings which tie your heart,
And make you sing with me.

It's oh so very dark
I hear you sing to me
Your voice across the park
A blissful melody.
If I could just be here
You know I'd sing your name
Take all the words I hear

And put them all to shame.
And I will play you like a harp,
Strum my fingers through your soul,
Pluck the strings which tie your heart,
And make you sing with me.

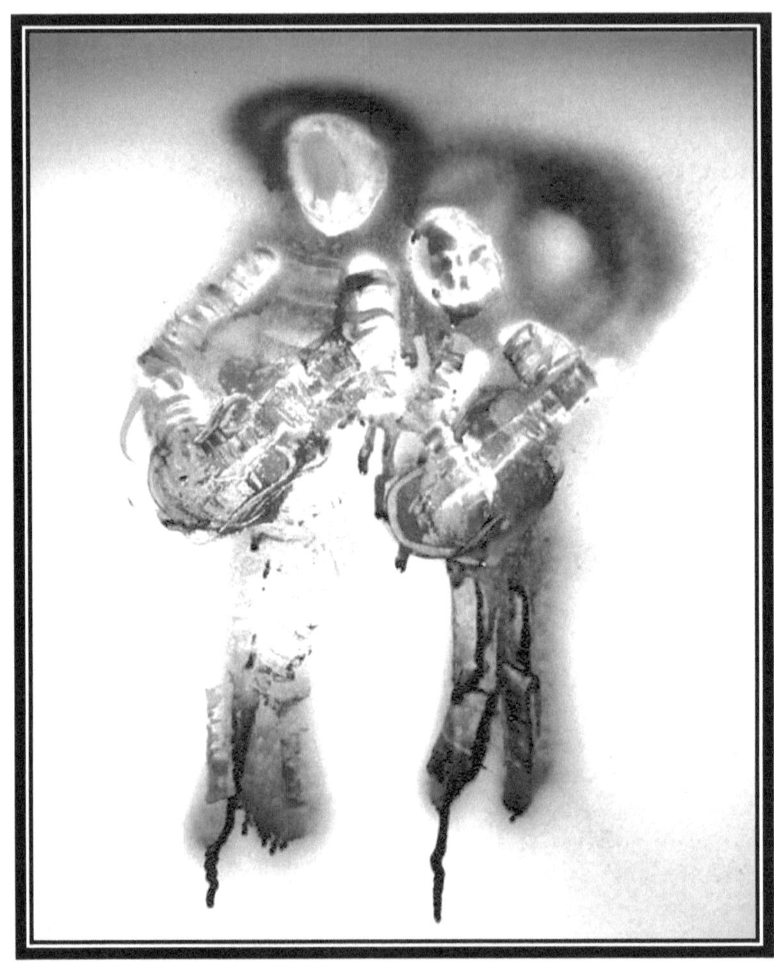

"Dueling Guitars"

Ody West

Espressive Ensemble

It wasn't that the musicians were distinct members, each their own god.
Instead they moved as a whole, an assembly of the creative,
The conductor acting as brain and architect.
An entire body in expressive, seamless choreography.

GIMME A BEAT

by RedCat

Gimme a beat
Make me tap my feet
Gimme a beat
Shake me out of this seat
Oh DJ, Gimme a beat
Make this night a treat

Vocals soar
Bass rumble
Modern attire crumble
Just like folk of old
When hand-drum music told
We're just here to stamp our feet
Dance the night away to this beat

Gimme a beat
Make me tap my feet
Gimme a beat
Make me leap this seat
Oh DJ, Gimme a beat
Make this room upbeat

Bodies sway
Bass rumble
Dancing emotions tumble
Just like folk of old
Dancing adulations, Spirits uphold
We're just here to stamp our feet
Dance all night until sunlit street

Gimme a beat
Make me tap my feet
Gimme a beat
Shake me out of this seat
Oh DJ, Gimme a beat
A night of dancing feet

SELFISH LULLABY

by Shane Windham

Hush, little baby
Please, stop growing up
Daddy's unprepared
for your coffee cup

I still see you
the way you see the moon;
beacon in the dark,
changing all too soon

Now, every new day
seems to hold less time
Won't be long till your books
don't even rhyme

Though grateful for the chance
to watch you grow,
I'm scared of the day I
must watch you go

For, it will mean that
my best times are done;
that we're past waking
as father and son

Still, hush, little baby
Sleep through the night
Daddy will make sure
everything's all right

LAID OUT ON THE BLACKTOP

by Layne Ambrose

Breathing in the lies
Has always been the same
Feel the darkness
Creeping in
Screaming in the dark
Hoping for a change in thought
Got to get the evil out
Purge myself from these thoughts
Laid out on the blacktop
Laying down as time forgot

Burning my own body at the stake
Witch, which demon am I today
Condemn all those with scars
Push them all so far
A fucking windup toy
For your amusement
Breathing in lies
Will always be the same
Living the way we were meant to be
Laid out on the blacktop
Laying down as time forgot

A breakdown was inevitable
Laughing your way to the grave
Was the only way
Learning to lean the right way
Swaying to the sound of the drums
The end was always nigh
For someone like me
Laid out on the blacktop
Laying down as time forgot
About someone like me

BESTIAL I BE

by Tristan Drue Rogers

See these teeth?
Canines louder than any nine
Of those called You

The devil's food for the demons
I choose to breathe in
HIS sins and crimes are the dots I've connected in my skull
Full my tummy be
Cursed elbows and toes
With bloody words and jurors
Have allowed me to walk into the club and dub myself
What they could never see me be

Bestial I be
Because my claws grew from kiddy paws
Oohs and awws tell me more by the screams that come after
Origami Spasms
Originality from spazzin'
Bodies in circles
It irked those
Who recognized me as a welcome mat
To yellow and all to mellow artists
Peace
Only after pieces
Are eaten
My nieces will never see me completed
I'll be in a jail cell

Hell is my voice
Hell is my voice
Hell is my choice

Bestial I be
Or am I just believing
That I am becoming
The work of art itself
Working harder than any artist
With no arms to paint could sell
I don't know me

Anger in the fangs that rang
As I reign in the pain of others
I wonder and want to wander away
I see those that fall and pray to nothing
That I could crawl to the wood
Of holy and stake my life
Yet a juicy steak is all the fakes
Will notice of me - No ticks atop my skin
As I lock myself away
Creating something that will
Carve my name into their tongues

Bestial I be
Be celestial, sell a bit
To get to the toll - Sell a tall tale
That lures you with currency
Fare well
Swell in the gel
Of bells and whistles
Wit only settles
As I swim in this land
My lungs fill with ether
And my lungs feel a puncture
The sum of my fears within your ears
I am here, where are you?
I be bestial
You just met me, you'll miss me soon
Soon playing to my tune
I be bestial
Soon playing to my tune

I am the prince
Awaiting the king - To wince
I be bestial
Soon playing to my tune
Scratching and gnawing at the neck
Of Cerberus
I be bestial
I be bestial
I be bestial
Ahh, now that is a fancy tune
Bestial

MENTALLY UNFIT TO BE ANYTHING BUT HUMAN

by Layne Ambrose

(Verse 1)
Creatures of habit
Digging a grave because that
Was the plan for today
Suicide was so much easier
When I had something to lose

(Pre-chorus)
What else could I be?
What is there really?

(Chorus)
Mentally unfit to be anything
Anything but human

(Verse 2)
Caught in a time loop
I was never meant to escape from
Digging at the stitches because that
Was the plan for today
Keeping up was so much easier
When I had something to care about
Caught myself staring at another grave
Wondering when it was going to be my time
Once again

(Pre-chorus)
What else could I be?
What is there really?

(Chorus)
Mentally unfit to be anything
Anything but human

(Verse 3)
Creatures we call human
Monsters we believe ourselves to be
Digging at the dirt, piece by piece
Was the plan all along
Just wish someone had told me
Gave me a shovel and not bloody knees
Caught the same disease in the end
Time always has a way to stick it in deeper
Mentally unfit to be anyone but me
Everything was so much easier
Before I learned the truth

(Outro/ Chorus)
Mentally unfit to be anything
Anything but human
What else could I be?
What is there really?
Anything, anything but human

TERPSICHORE

by A. P. Christopher

There, in worlds of weeping fog she dances
Hand in hand, a court of masks and gloves
Gown of winter white
A countenance to steal your sight
From even momentary glances
So when sleeping, she is all you're dreaming of

Sweeping through each moment, she entrances
Angels gather high to sing of her
Scribing newer hymns
For now the older ones are dim
When even heaven she enhances
So imposing, even kings approach demure

Spiraling, she moves so elegantly
Even seasons stop to so behold
She in such display
Who is December, dressed in May
When lips of August smile gently
'Neath her hair of mid-July, all wrapped in gold

Music is the sound of her composure
Even now, I wait for just a chance
Knowing not of faith
But still a captive to her grace
My heart and soul forever chose her
Hoping once to ask her, "May I have this dance?"

THIS USED TO BE MY PLAYGROUND

by Cassa Bassa

We never had a photo together
yet I remember every expression of you
I have never returned the books you left on my bookshelf
the only ones without dust
Silent night has never been peaceful
since I heard your car burned into flames
on the highway with extra snow
buried your seventeen years old charred body

This used to be my playground
This used to be my childhood dream
This used to be the place I ran to whenever I was in need of a friend
Why did it have to end

I have never been able to say goodbye to you
maybe that is why nothing good had been with you

You left me a letter before you boarded the plane
You know I have never opened it to this day
Nothing matters really since the day you've been gone

This used to be my playground
This used to be my childhood dream
This used to be the place I ran to whenever I was in need of a friend
Why did it have to end

Nothing is as pure as childhood sweetheart
No love is sweeter than sweet sixteen

I dream of you still in black and white
Your linen shirt flying on the swing
Your manic laughter on the seesaw

This used to be my playground
This used to be my childhood dream
This used to be the place I ran to whenever I was in need of a friend
Why did it have to end

There is no he will ever replace you
In the land of the living
You are my perfection
my first and my destiny

HOW DO YOU GO ON?

By Layne Ambrose

Your need in me to die
Bleed me out slowly
Had me on my knees
Walking through glass
Each piece sharper than the last
Don't assume because I'm dead
That I am gone
Screaming the words into a death hollow song
Gave you all that you wanted
What you need and what was left for me
In my shell I shall rot
A victim of myself
How do you go on?
Living like this?

Waiting on blackened lungs
Pushing the glass deeper
I'll always beg for more
Hate myself more than you could
Ever imagine, how I go on
I am the greatest and worst
Thing ever born in this world
A machine whose self-infliction is me
Call me whatever you may
Screaming the words into a death hollow song
Gave you all that you wanted
What you needed and what was left for me
In my shell I shall rot
How do you go on?
Living like this?

I hide in the smile, behind your eyes
Piece by piece I will always be
Here to remind you that I am me and you are you
So run, hide, doesn't matter when I'm
Buried in your mind
Block me out, numb me down, play the game
But know all I've got is time
Burying myself deeper and deeper in you
Tell me how do you go on?

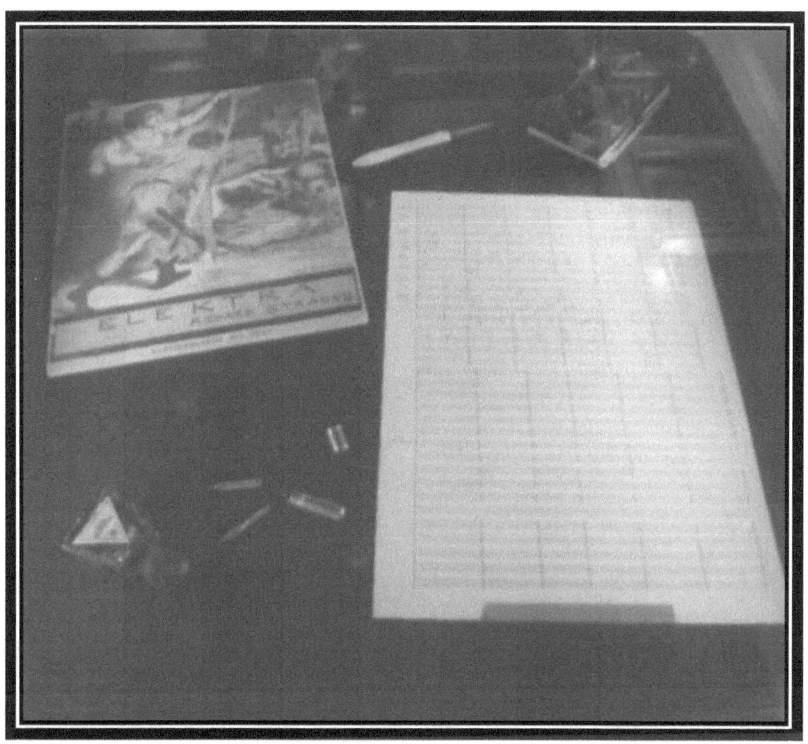

Richard Strauss (1864-1949)

His writing desk and accoutrements at Villa Christina, Garmisch-Partenkirchen, Bavaria, Germany.

The piano edition of his opera Elektra is in the top left.

Photograph: S J Reizlein

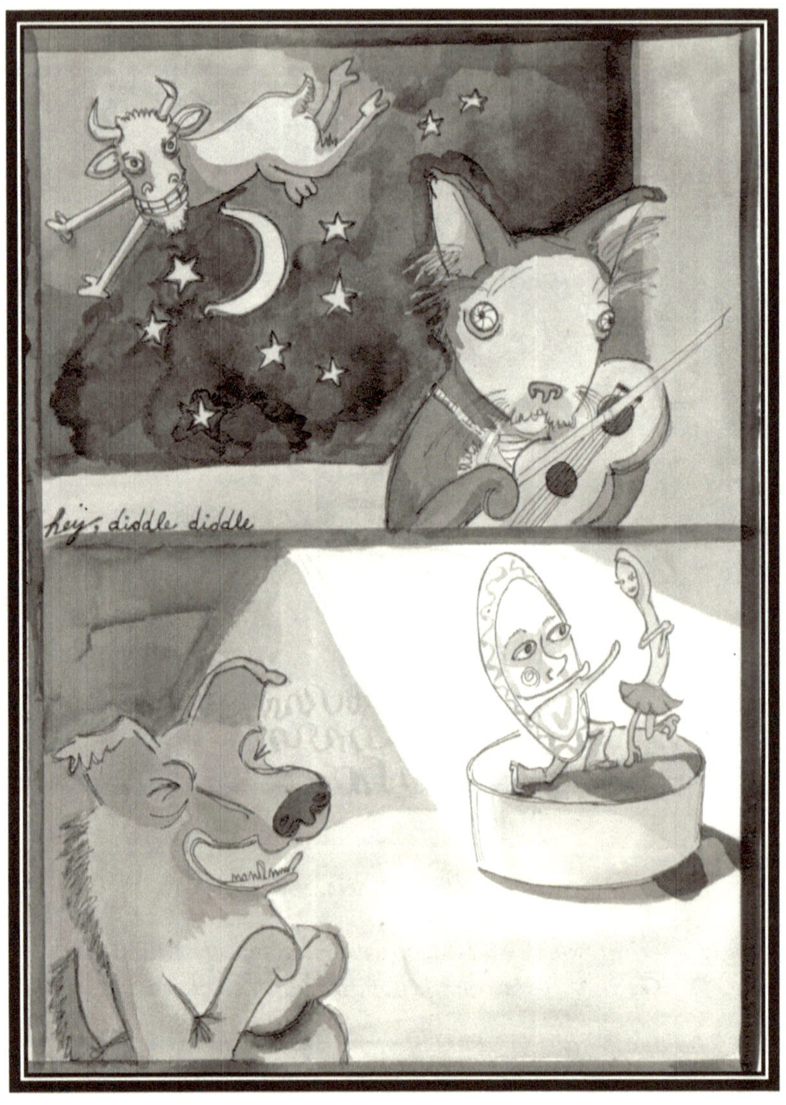

"hey diddle diddle"

emje mccarty

AH! POMME, POMME, POMMET

(Three Songs, after Claire Isabelle Geo Pommet (Pomme))

by S J Reizlein

Ah! Pomme, Pomme, Pommet,
it is impossible to look upon you without
seeing a fresco beauty, with a male gaze,
female gaze or any gaze imaginable,
yes, you are a Klimt model holding a harp,
tousled hair, dark, far away contemplation.

Pomme, Pomme, Pommet, you would adorn, with
melodic grace, the Beethoven frieze, and before
an altar in a Belgian church, your strings
shimmer electricity, an angel's air, of *Birds,*
skinny, long, still stance, gamine,
auto-harp minstrel sensuality

Pomme, Pomme, Pommet, a sad song of
craved motherhood, in an imaginary world
you create, banshee choral wails flicker, arch
and fall, amid the voices of children,
the unrelenting tick-tock of a biological clock,
a dismal worry of child-filled existence,
as *Grandiose* reverie.

Pomme, Pomme, Pommet, sings of loss,
of the blank stare of old age,
when the mind forgets,
the inexorable beat of time passes
from youth into senility,
life's *Light* dissipates, to look the same
but be someone else, to not recognize
those for whom we once breathed love,
to leave, while unconscious of living

A FOOL'S MASQUERADE

by Robert Birkhofer

[VERSE 1]
Where should I go
When I don't even know where to start?
And what should I do
When everything is falling apart?
I've been in love for a long, long time
With the way you make me smile
And I've been dreaming every single night
About you all the while
But I've been crying 'cause I miss you
And I can't seem to let you go
Yeah, I'm dying just to kiss you
And I wanted you to know
That there's a time and a place
Where we all make mistakes
Because we're all so caught up
In running the race
And there's a feeling I get
When I look to the west
I still see you walking off down that road all by yourself
Now everyday I'm drowning in regret
Tell me—did you feel right after you left?
I don't think I could bear to see you with anybody else

[CHORUS]
If I could trade words written on a page
For your precious, golden heart
I'd fill a hundred journals
With a hundred rhapsodies
And if notes drawn upon a staff
Could end the time we've spent apart
I'd fill a hundred scores
With a hundred symphonies
But I'm a fool masquerading as a musician
Who wishes his life had been written
In lead instead of unforgiving ink
And I know my trifling songs
Can't erase the reasons you're gone
So, please excuse a fool while he sings

[VERSE 2]
Where did you go
After you left me alone in the dark?
And what did you do
With the two broken halves of my heart?
If I'm gonna move on in a world where you're gone
I'm gonna need that broken heart back
But I can't fight the truth—my heart belongs to you
No matter if it's in pieces or intact
I remember sunny days
Of warmth and love that knew no fear
But when the winter came, you walked away
And now I need you to hear
That there's a time, looking back
When we were moving too fast
When we were too blind to see
All the good things going past
And there's a feeling I get
When I see your photograph
I still hear all the tears you cried after I did you wrong
Do you think that I don't know?
Do you think I wanted you to go?
Now all I can do is say I'm sorry in a song

[CHORUS]

[BRIDGE]
I'll burn through the pain
Of another endless day
Where the sky's just the same
Plain shade of gray
Holding onto a dream
That our love was meant to be
Can't you see you're all I need?
Can you please come back to me?

[CHORUS]

I KNOW

by Layne Ambrose

(Verse)
Some of the darkest thoughts
Have come since I said I forgive you
With the water in my lungs
The skin falls off and I wonder
Is this right?

(Pre-Chorus)
Walking dead, living a life, or going through
What I deserve now?

(Chorus)
I know, I know, I know now

(Verse 2)
I love you doesn't hold the same weight
As before, driving a nail between
The wall of me and you
A silence that slowly kills
What words are real and the rest made up
Somedays I feel like running
Others I feel moored in place
Stuck between how it is and how it was
Black door opened in my mind
Shut but not closed

(Pre-Chorus)
Confusion has set in and doubt consumes me
Is this right?
Walking dead, living a life, or going through
What we deserve now?

(Chorus)
I know, I know, I know now

(Verse 3)
Lost and confused choking down words
Same as before but something, some things
Have changed
Water fills my lungs and then I think
I know
Life consumes me and then I think
I know
Life gets in the way and then I think
I knew nothing at all
A reminder of how I've always been
Then, before, or now

(Outro)
I know, I know, I know now

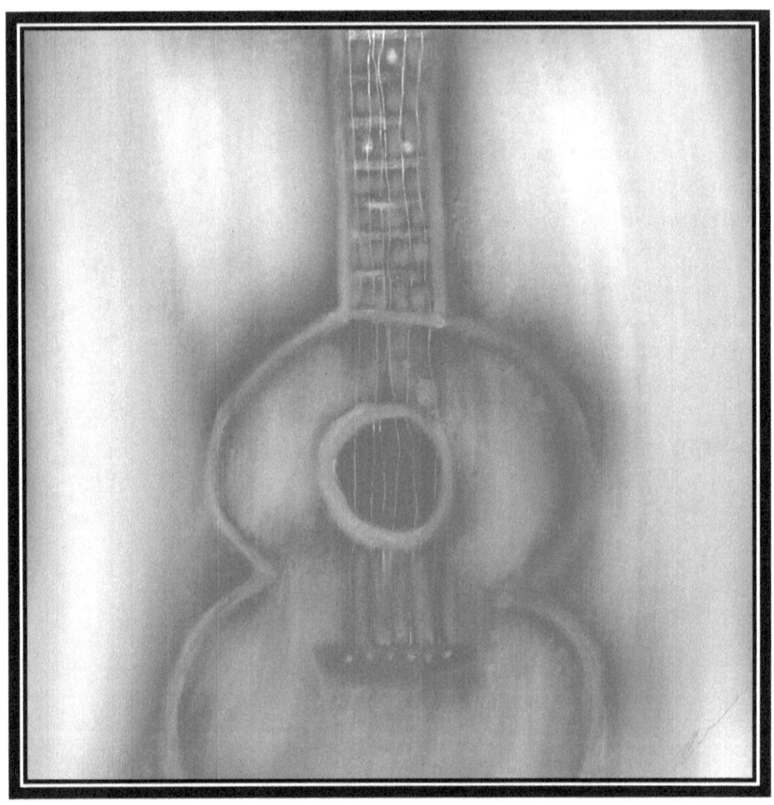

"Broken Strings"

Brandon White

Diminuendo

There was, after a time, though we could not say how long,
A lessening, a loosening of the grip.
The music had held sway, influence.
A quiet, almost melancholy, settled in all around us.

REPEAT

by River Dixon

There is a rhythm to everything
Sometimes felt, not often heard

In my dreams, which are plenty
Are found the substance
Within the meter
Flailing along frequencies
Too loud to comprehend
A bitter crescendo
Falling short of climax
Before cresting on
An utter reprise
Too distant to recall
A tempo, rise and fall

Bow my head
To thunderous applause
As everyone loves a tragedy
Jeering with demand
For not an encore
But a repeat performance

AN ODE TO SEEKING SOMETHING CLOSE TO FITTING IN

by M Ennenbach

i wish
to curl up
bend my limbs
into
a fibonacci sequence
find nature
in the unnatural
recombinant strands
of innocent abuse

a simple
pavlovian response
to the indecent
orchestral arraignments
drifting on the theorems
of the bell curve
the bell jar
the latent depression
of existence

crack
my painful joints
into whatever
patent pending
disgraceful ballet
that soothes
the sultry sighs
of irregular
unregulated regurgitants

we are all art
crafted
from the scraps
of anecdotal drippings
coursing
in chaotic array
to the pulse
of the uncaring
cosmos themselves

seeking the pulse
of unseen organs
spewing
the last rhythmic notes
of an insular
composition
the wheezing sighs
of woodwind throats
singing into the abyss

FEBRUARY 10, 1976

by Braeden Michaels

I didn't mean what I said
when I said you meant nothing to me
I couldn't stand the agony
knowing I was treated like a chorus
You played me over and over
to only find yourself dancing in spite
You bask in my discomfort
and relish in the irritation
I left my sorrow on February 10, 1976
Time was my only friend
Change was the only selection
Perception was my sidewalk
Clarity is subjective
and fear was my song
The date is a tattoo on my arm

SAD SONGS

by emje mccarty

you know that broken heart
i keep
in a jar
on my bedside table?
seems it's flown away
on new butterfly
wings
just flown away
and now
when sad songs
play
on the radio
i look inside me
and think
"huh…
i got nuthin'."

SATURDAY MORNING

by Piano Girl

Late morning cup of coffee
Favorite blue jeans and
James Taylor t-shirt
Quiet music playing
In the background
My busy thoughts
Speeding toward
The upcoming week
While simultaneously
Revisiting the previous
Another sip of coffee
Suddenly I remember
Today is Saturday
Time to breathe
Slow my thoughts
Allow difficult moments
To become tiny specks
Obscured by splashes
Of bright colors
On a large canvas
A reflective painting
Of the past week
Where encouraging moments
Cause trying ones to fade
All on a Saturday morning

CENSORSHIP DEFAULT

by Layne Ambrose

Took the only road ahead
Land of the living, world of the dead
Walking along the side, the edge
Dancing in the overflow
Been told I have a way with words
Vulgar, honest, truth, sidetracked
Out of view from the world
Lost idea buried under regret
Gave a mountain of
Something I can't say
I've been told self-censorship
Is the hardest thing to overcome
Broken filter, speak my mind
Because I don't give a ____ about you
How you feel…
How I am not about how you feel
Hold it back, lock it up, who I am when I'm not
Hidden, discarded idea of who I am
Who I should be…
High road looking down
So small like ants on the ground
Want to jump but then again I've always been
Willing to fall…
Unglued view, unhinged and worst of all
Been thinking a lot like you
Now I'm down in it
Views have been reversed
Perspective is a bitch
Covered in your shit
Discarded left behind
Fits like a glove, my first and second skin
As the shit drips from my lips
Knew there was no censorship default
Built within me at all

THE HOOK OF NOWHERE

by Shane Windham

I wanted to leave you a playlist behind
when I passed on;
its working title was nothing more
than the words 'dead lover'
And, the deeper I dug myself into those
dark places beneath the blare,
the more I felt you were already listening
Toward the end, I even believed that you
might come to my rescue

With only a full day left before
our now-meaningless anniversary,
I purposely dulled my other senses
Nothing but the music fed me there in the dark
A mere 87 minutes is what our
retrospective amounted to,
and, hour after hour, I let myself imagine
how it might feel to go back in time;
to live us all over again

I wondered if, in this process of condensing
the length of our intertwined travels,
I'd somehow forgotten a magical moment or two
Perhaps you'd recollect, and ponder over
the broken impossibility of such an absence

Wholly unaware of the time, I fell asleep
in that repetition of tears I'd tired of living,
but the pieces never stopped performing
I dreamt of your sensual piano playing,
and awoke to Chopin's 'Ocean' emptying
as though predicting the coming finality
of my ears being able to hear it

A few quick nicks amid the noise,
then the world started to fade
And, only as I began to disappear
did the grotesque chorus of truth
come screeching into my head
like broken glass in a car crash:
There's so much that would be new to me
which I'll never get to hear,
and you aren't even interested in listening
to all that's going to be left of me

THE GHOSTS BETWEEN THE NOTES

by Brandon White

"Do you have to subject the rest of us to this?"
she says with a smile,
as Lonesome Blues plays softly
over the car stereo.

I know she's saying it in jest,
but I also know she'd prefer
to listen to something,
anything else.

I try to explain my appreciation for
what she's hearing.
I tell her it's not just the music,
it's that we're listening to history!

That these people,
probably long dead,
gathered together
to make this recording.

These people had friends,
and lovers and children.
These people had terrible
regrets and small victories.

That's why I listen.
To hear the ghosts between
the notes.
I know that sounds pretentious.

The truth is that when I hear
this music, I hear a time
before the pain and complication
of recent years.

I hear a world where my father
is alive and vital, his whole life
stretched out before him.
Long before cancer,

before shot nerves.
Long before everyone
thought their opinion
held weight in my life.

Long before grief
and random breakdowns.
Long before simplicity
was a memory.

EFFLORESCENCE

by Mark Ryan

Do you feel the change in weather?
The heart beating for the very first time.
Get down on the ground and listen to the soil.
The trumpeting pound of nature's pride.
Beating like a dominance in my body.
Listen to my flesh as the drumbeat breathes and sighs.
You turn a season within, devoid of the frost of winter.
Bathed in only the crystal glaze of summer.
Always sunny when you look my way.
A twice look biscuit fire that scorches my soul.
And sets alight a rhythm that cannot be contained.
But I do not burn, I bloom.
Mesmerized and polarized in the dew drops of your joy.
The pounding of the flowers in the spring of your step.
The noise lifts from the crevices and sets my mind to dance.
Thump as the earth shakes.
Gasp with each breath.
Gardening in twilight as you sleep when I wake.

CROSSING NONTRANSFERABLE TERRITORY

by J Matthew Waters

you could hear bad moon rising
coming from the other room
the music somewhat muffled
fogerty's voice unmistakable

stepping outside
it was pretty much the same
excluding the music and that
unmistakable voice
transitioning into inner nonsense

at the next stop
glass tri-fold doors open
exposing old men sitting on
metal benches
stitching together wounds
inflicted half a world away

speakers on light poles
suddenly become charged
casting shadows and
sounding alarms disguised
as folk rock from the sixties

trading wheels for wings
up up and away you go
defeating gravity and
orbiting unfamiliar rhythms
bursting above the clouds

DEATH COMES TO THE OPERA

by S J Reizlein

There are many ways lovers
can die on stage,
when Death comes to the opera.

There is the blade to the guts,
for the Seville gypsy girl.
Rejected suitor's keen knife, beware,
he will take your life.

Meanwhile, in Japan, life in ruins,
honour-bound to purge her shame,
with paternal sharp steel, by her
own hand, broken on a wheel
a Butterfly died, Pinkerton's
ditched teenage bride.

Confusion reigns, two kids,
in old Verona, swig poison,
plunge a dagger, dual suicide-woe,
their star-crossed last liaison

Burn, Brünnhilde baby, burn,
it may be magic fire,
but she suffers for love,
Valhalla is aflame,
the old gods' funeral pyre.

Pathology of white plague,
pale camellia handkerchiefs
turn red, lungs
eject a cough-up spree,
congested ends for the courtesan
and cold-hand Mimi.

Elektra indulgent, death dance ecstasy,
suitable end to a gory orgy; and
Senta falls for a Flying Dutchman sailor,
tumbles, a selfless lemming-sea-dive
saves his soul, lifts the old curse,
though she is not permitted to survive

Let us end this wretched, deep mourning trawl,
with the greatest love's death of them all.
Romeo and Juliet for grown-ups,
bereft Isolde sings to dead Tristan,
senses him in all of nature,
in the world's breath,
still alive, Cornish passion,
her unbounded zest,
seeks out of life where
there is only death,
it all concludes no
happier than the rest,
when Death comes to the opera

THE GLOW CONSPIRES

by Tristan Drue Rogers

The glow conspires to illuminate,
Beyond its ability
The song conspires to have melody,
Only it's too late
That grinning man conspires to deceive, theft, death: the rich given disease
The poor conspire to rob the rich,
Yet we just rob ourselves and they laugh at it
The dove is innocent so she can't conspire,
Long as you take care of her like a child,
Because if you don't that glow will fade,
She'll find another socket that just might behave
The song is a nightmare put in the vast lasting pit of rhymes,
But it can't be found since you ain't hearin' more than a beat this time,
So discuss the lust that you wish us would just abandon upon dusk,
Too bad it's just the sad and dead that live long enough to reach your earbuds
Cuz these new grinning folks are jokes poking at your earlobes pretending that they ain't bred from
wealth or intelligence even though they never walked that tightrope of poverty or read a book
Overtly, we chose this path and at last it came true - hip hop ain't the underdog, we're the truth,
But if that truth says do all the drugs and get fucked up, blame your homies for what you done, sending
them to incarceration, while you out here havin' fun
Then who are you, kid, glaring at the sun,
You became darkness
You illuminatin' none.
The day will come when you best prepare to run,
we chasing you, cuz you don't represent no one.
For that life is for the disposed, the collateral
The impractical supposed radical that instead chose addiction
In lieu of the righteous words originators were spittin'
You ain't your only witness
We see you and to us it's sickening
Time to learn from history, children
Not spit upon it, crumblin' the buildings we built
But nah, you ain't even listenin'
Tumbling underneath a mountain of filth
You destroyed the progress and appeals

Met with the mobsters of commerce and that's real
Mumblin' about nonsense without a sound that's yours
You just screech and the auto tune is there to repurpose
Find something to say, you don't
Guess I'll go my way, you just go...
the grin conspires to deceive
The song desires a melody
The dove no longer chooses right, she chooses what helps feed her kids at night
The glow strobes to an illumination
And we all out here, with out minds, struggling for rations...

OFF-KEY RAGE

by Shane Windham

I once thought I knew you well,
but then I heard the hidden broadcast
of songless people crying their last
within your deepest layers
Your harmonies disguise the dissonance
of that maniac found within;
those auto-tuned insides

Somebody has to stop your progression;
and, since I'm the only one who knows what you are,
it seems the spotlight is awaiting us
Recognize that it was you who once assured me,
"Scream loud enough, and people
will mistake your pain for melodic art."
Thus, I will use your breaking body
to be thought the master of my craft

The drumming in us both intensifies
as I strike you like a chord
This is how it feels to be on the receiving end
of a dedication which aims
to thieve your world of signals
This is the intrusive and unplanned
commotion you forced on others;
that tune playing beneath the headphones
which you couldn't be bothered
to experience for yourself

My needle continues to cut you as you spin
Your blood pours down on both of us
like a hard rain spilling over fresh lava;
I watch it pool in your grooves,
and wonder how many singers will be saved
by the destruction of just this one—
perhaps the saddest song would sing
of such a necessity

My voice, however, is inaudible
as I await the final pitch of your ashes
And, I now believe it safe to say
that the saddest songs
go unsung for good reason
For, we are here to offer tomorrow
proof of yesterday,
and all you ever did was rob
the here and now of its hits

MUSE SICK

by M Ennenbach

as I lay, shaking with fever beneath the thick comforter that gives no comfort, lost in dream, lost in song
music soothes the savage beast
or so they say
but nothing soothes a broken heart
miles plays softly in the background as the world seems off axis, my world has flipped hemispheres, I am lost
sorrow swirls among the saxophone notes, a back beat ringing the bop with aching reverberation
muse sick assaults my soul and mind
without mercy, without stop
the world gone hollow without her smile
I wonder, in my sickness if this common, if the joy being snuffed like a candle, has ever affected the greats like this
If they ever lost their muse, stopped hearing the music resonating in their minds, in their hearts, in their souls
music enrages the empty golem
or so I have seen
and nothing soothes a broken heart
so I lay, shivering with fever that wells not from illness but from the withdrawal of her smile, tempered by muse sickness
miles plays on but I no longer hear

THE BRIDGE QUIVERS IN THE DARK

by Braeden Michaels

Strumming the heartache like it's falling rain
Tearing into the sea of my everlasting sorrow
Pouring out my agony in a gut-wrenching ballad
Spotlight shines on my frozen emptiness
Wrapped up in shivers and anguish in the chorus

Overwhelming silence stood like fog in these walls
Sipping on unlimited fear and deep colors of strain
Overtaken by the river of bitterness
Recognizing twelve ounce drops of sympathy
And the bridge quivers in the dark

"Love broke me into a thousand pieces
Left me as a shadow that no one can see"

Drenched by the sweet melancholy in my voice
Sadness vibrates through the microphone
Dressed in sentimental rhymes and reckless words
Thresholds of my soul ignited by sour coals
Buried in the chill and screams in the chorus

Cloaked in sedatives and a stage name
Tasting the hollow joys of acclamation
Fading into the sunrise of sheet music
Drowning in a burnt and invisible treasures
And the bridge quivers in the dark

"Love broke me into someone I can't recognize
Left me as a shadow with brokenness filled in my eyes"

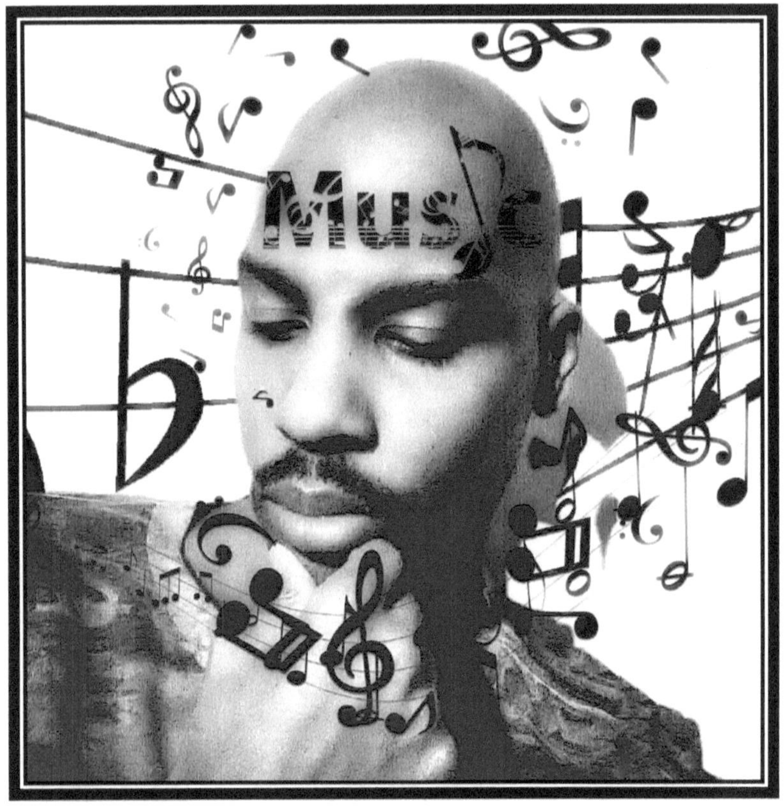

"Meditation on Music"

Leon Jones

Finale

And before we were fully aware, even cognizant of what was happening,
His fingers, as if holding a thread, pulled taut.
The music abruptly ended and we sat in stunned silence.
Even now, much later, the nostalgia of that moment endures in our hearts.

SUCH TUNES AS THESE

by Chris Nelson

We ran and ran
And sang the songs
That echoed in
Our virgin minds,
That grew our core
And saw the notes
The melodies
Beneath our feet,
The words you sang
That rang with truth
Brought meaning to
Our youthful lives,
Each chord that played
And stayed on ears
Brought open doors
And dead-end tears,
Salt-water rush
And blush to cheek
But still we sang
To birth the smile,
In given time
The rhyme touched those
With younger souls
Than we could hold,
Our ears reached out
No doubt inside
That we would hear
Such tunes again.

AS BEAUTIFUL AS

by Candice Louisa Daquin

As beautiful as that moment after one has passed, reminding you
of red leaves intercepted with green
of water dripping silently outside a window in the morning fog
of love creeping into your heart like a slow-remembered dream
of friendship found, unexpectedly
of fears that dissolve momentarily and allow in the light
of dreams on the froth, dancing
I want to dance
I want to dance so badly
I want to sway with the music pulsing over me
like red lights and purple
of the babies I don't have
the people then and now
of faces I will not see again
of my own life short and long
of that bookshop that closed down
that used to stock great poetry
of those shoes I bought and always wore
until they hurt my feet too much
of Ireland and Ruth's green cardigan
piercing our ears because we liked the man who did it
eating lemons with our beer
years ahead years behind
babies in our womb, sadness in our minds
futures written on concrete and soil
one forever, the other grows into a tree
of love the first time and the last
thinking into the future, forgetting the past
tumbling down as the leaves shed and fall
my mother's absence
my father's quiet presence
one there, one gone
switched around
switched around like a merry-go-round
horses painted bright
like candlelight
in a forest without a view
a corridor to walk down
where is the light?
where is the dancer?
where is my child?

where is my lover?
where do I turn?
Letting go of her hand I spin
faster, faster to the sound of GOA
and Eastern song
my ancestry
my bond
I love this
I hate this
I fear this
I want this life
as beautiful as
I am

BIRD OF PREY

by ValentinA Saldaña

Once upon a time
I believed in you
I wrote fairy tales of wonder

I revisit you
when I least expect
I journey back
to our horizon

Then a bird of prey
circles round my
head
and I kill
those lies of Eden

Scenes of earth and sky
flood my mind with jars
of unsaid words
unspoken

I wonder
where you are
as I walk alone
along the shores
of kind nostalgia

Then a bird of prey
circles round my
head,
and I kill
those lies of Eden

I think of going back
to the place we were
right before I left you

Angst of our past
don't seem so bad
for a moment
I surrender

Then a bird of prey
circles round my
head,
and I kill
those lies of Eden

I WILL SPEAK OF THIS

by Candice Louisa Daquin

of this difficulty that cannot be summed,
of this poem that bursts from me and is never written.

Of the desert, and its blankness,
of the dead rattle snake as we drive 90 mph through tarmac
watching death collect on the side of the road.

I will speak of seeing the blue mountains
the smoke and mist collecting at the head and hiding the tips.

I will speak of seeing the emptiness,
something that once filled me with hope,
when I thought I would redeem,
when I thought I had time, and life ahead,
when I thought things would take life again like a bird sleeping to wake.

But this time I only felt the emptiness,
the solitary motion of space shifting in front of me,
the empty road,
and my own smallness in it.

I saw that the city contained for me the escape
that I have long been suffering under,
and while it is vile and vacuous, it is real for me,
as the burst of music is, and the dance.

BYE BYE AMERICAN PIE

by J Matthew Waters

where did all the songs go
the ones once playing in my head
when I needed them most

paused without incidence
abruptly held hostage in the cloud
silenced at gunpoint

the day the music died
sadly becoming a daily occurrence
offline and in the streets

I've practiced enough drills
to last a second or third lifetime
yet somehow the songs
never seem to make it out alive

MELODY

by A. P. Christopher

Your melody - a wind chime with a sad, familiar tune
Where winds were always waning and the sun was never strong
Like light that offered patterns from a slowly waning moon
And like a ship upon the waves
That chased the moon for what it gave
I tried to match your tempo, but could never sing along

Your melody - a bell that never held a pure sustain
Where storms were ever roaring and the sky was mottled blue
As if it wore the weight of all the rain that never came
And so umbrellas we forgot
What once we were, and yet were not
I tried to brave the weather, but it's just so hard to do

Your melody - a hand that, long ago, was pulled away
Where fingertips were reaching for a hope that faded out
And lips were left unmoving, never knowing what to say
Until the words were lost to time
As if a note from distant chimes
I tried to find the music that could banish all the doubt

Your melody - a sound that, even now, feels like a wound
Where epithets are whorls upon the fingers typing still
On keys that play a song that, even now, grows out of tune
From fingers that have lost their way
And lips that only know to say
I tried. I really tried. But pen and ink just can't convey the way I feel.

SEASHORE LULLABY

by Mark Tulin

Every summer, Aunt Mary took me to Atlantic City.
We strolled past the majestic hotels
with rose and tulip gardens
that flowered in our memories.

We walked the creaky boards
in our sandaled feet.
We watched the men push the tourists
in the rolling chairs.

We ate funnel cakes
and chocolate marshmallow fudge.
We went to the pier and laughed
at the monkey banging symbols
and playing a squeezebox tune.

Herman's Hermits sang *There's a Kind of Hush.*
Martha and the Vandellas, *Dancing in the Street.*
The diving horse climbed the 90-foot ladder,
scaling the heavens, jumping into a pool of water.

We stayed on the boards till the sun went down.
We smelled of clams on the half shell,
slept with the soothing sound of rolling waves,
and a big brass band in the distance
playing a seashore lullaby.

MUSIC BOX

by ValentinA Saldaña

ballerina beauty
where have you gone
little box misses you
still plays your song
you kept my trinkets
you stored my sweets
you held my fantasies
hear them they weep
i sleep now in satin
surrounded by wood
i would follow your trail
if only i could
diamond dust gathers
around all my dreams
no, nothing is ever
as good as it seems

ENAMORED

by CG Tenpenny

Like beaten steel, I am hammered.

A steel drum, the pannist's clamor,
stutter, stumble, and stammer.

Syncopate and sing for you,
the best beats are lost and left out, too.

Incomplete, arrhythmic, it
beats against the bone,
on the "one-and,"
it is clear that the pannist
plays alone.

But, the pannist still hammers
against my ribs,
'ever clamoring his angry,
discordant standard.

It is a song meant for you.

It hurts to hear, but listen -
the two is never missing,
because, as with you,

I am enamored

by the drum-beat's truth.

AT THE WORLD'S END

by emje mccarty

at the world's end
i think
most of all
i will miss
long drives
on
winding country roads
rippling
in and out of sunshine
shade trees
hanging low
and impossibly
green against the sky
impossibly blue
clouds speckling
the road ahead
driving too fast
sometimes
windows
down
music
loud
always

WHERE IS THE HOUR?

by Candice Louisa Daquin

Where is the hour? The hem, falling away, out of reach, bending to, catch, far, too far from grasp, where has, this stitch, loosening in hours, uncovered, keep?

Still I see you there, standing in fallen light, extinguished by time, roaring in fitted yell across wet eyes, closing, closet yourself in years like forgotten photos vanish in fire

Walking toward you, my voice hoarse, we have aged, once holding me low, you step with strength, pulling my arc behind you, whispered dance in thick gowns, rustling like secrets on silent floors, pluck music taut

It aches deep in my skin to hold you tightly above waves, as rushing forward and back, we form silhouettes against emerging earth

If, after so long, our dark need shadows still, in smooth lean, move gently, a fastened slip from one into another, burning in soft fire, time is thief when forgetful we stare into mirrors, we rush to amend by memory, that wakeful motion under spotlight

ALL FOR FREE

(L Cohen at Eastnor Castle, 2008)

by S J Reizlein

see Leonard Cohen, all for free, and there you are
the other side of a fence, here in quintessential,
rural England, beneath the Malvern Hills,
no security, well none we see, and the climb
is easy, even for me, in these castle camp grounds,
though it's all a showy, nineteenth century folly

and here you are, dark suit, that hat you have adopted,
a bow, a flourish to the audience, you really have become
a gentleman troubadour, oracle, a hip grandfather,
a sing-along to all your hits, Montreal meets jovial Merry England,
you flash a twinkle eye to all new Mariannes, Suzannes
and Sisters of Mercy, I hope you remember them all well

because they likely remember you well, as mean-spirited,
at times, you left your muse, yes, it's art for art's sake,
your creative juices an excuse, poor way to ease a lover's
heartache, hey that's no way to say goodbye, Marianne
forgave you, so that's OK, that last letter you sent her proved
that you're the man, so all your trespasses are wiped clean

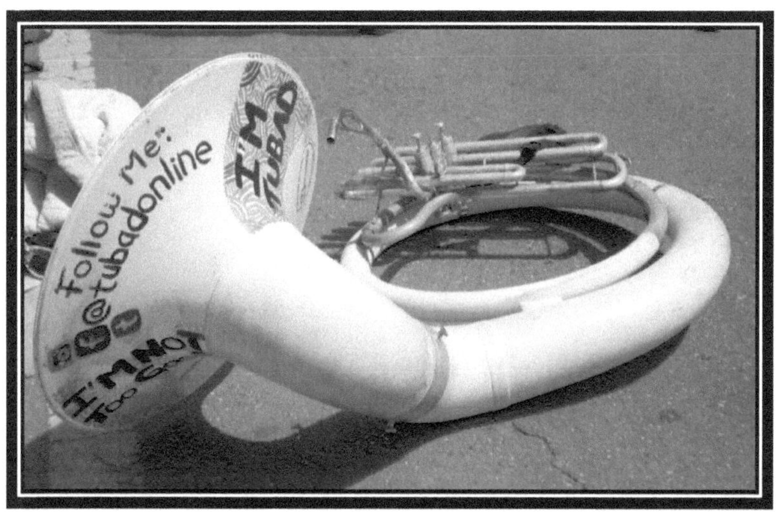

"I'm Not Too Good, I'm Tubad"

Easter Parade, New Orleans

Photograph: Janet Sawatsky

WHISKEY IN THE JAR

by J Matthew Waters

monday in july
midday sun weighs on my
mundane thoughts
oscillating fan stuck on low
collar unbuttoned and stained
wandering thoughts leading me
to wonder what the night will bring

there's whiskey in the jar
within arm's reach
reminding me of old irish songs
and heavy metal music
taking me back to the summer
of nineteen seventy-eight
when days were so much simpler

BLUE CHEVY VEGA

by Mark Tulin

Circa 1971.
I'm a teenager with a bad case of acne.
I'm driving a brand-new blue Chevy Vega,
delivering groceries from a kosher deli.

A Horse with No Name is playing on the radio
as I circle the streets of my desert.
My teenage emotions running high
like the sounds of the music I play.

I'm driving in third gear down a tar-covered street,
stopping briefly to deliver bags to the elderly,
speeding past mowed lawns and brick row homes,
cherubs and gargoyles seven-feet high.

I turn off Penny Lane
past city blocks brimming with rosy faces,
children hitting whiffle balls into the sun.
Mothers humming pop tunes to their stroller babies.
My life connected to the same AM station.

MY TIME AMONG THE IMMORTALS

by Brandon White

I'd be lying if I said
that I don't miss
the simplicity of
the old days.

It's funny,
they didn't seem so
simple at the time.
Boy, was I spoiled.

The buzz of the neon,
the haze of cigarette smoke
that stung your eyes and
burned your nose.

The ache of my fingers
as I began the third or fourth set.
How soothing the cold beer felt
on my tired throat.

For most musicians,
this is the existence they settle into.
Probably not what they dreamed of,
but it's what they get.

I almost feel weird calling myself
a musician anymore.
Maybe I'm just a writer.
Maybe that's all I ever was.

Who knows, people bought
my tunes, and I still get
the occasional mailbox money.
I guess that means something.

There were things about it
I loathed and still do.
Like having promotional
photos taken.

Nothing says I'm a legitimate
artist quite like staring
into the distance
with a serious expression.

I always found the hats
and beards amusing as well.
Hipster bullshit
from your next American Idol.

I'm being an asshole.
It's just that I'd like to see more
attention to craft
and less to what's cool.

Cool is always fleeting,
changing form, subject to the times.
Great art transcends cool.
Time is powerless against it;

And it's all around us!
And Rolling Stone knows nothing of it!
And TMZ knows nothing of it!
And the industry knows nothing of it!

It's in a smokey dive
on a wooden stool
being belted out by the best
damn singer you've never heard,

and drowned out
by the blonde in the front row
who thinks the whole damn bar
cares about how her day went.

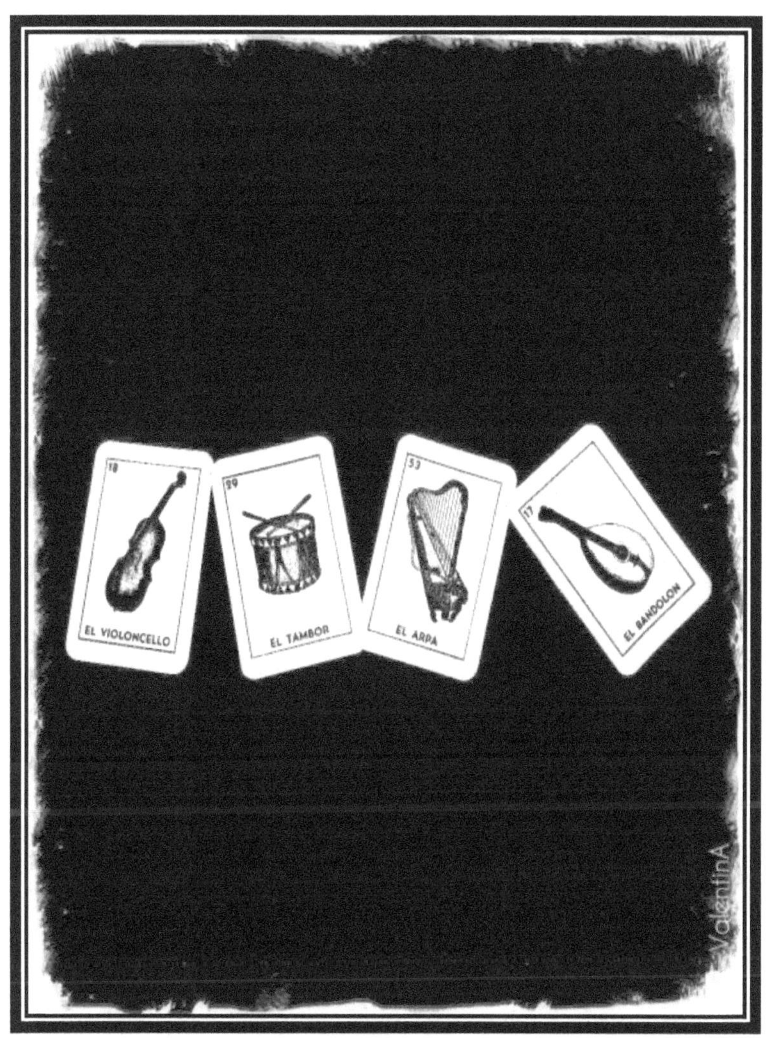

"Cuatro Tarjetas (Four Cards)"

ValentinA Saldaña

CONTRIBUTORS

A.P. CHRISTOPHER writes poetry, short stories, and novels.
Blog: Constant Variable at constantvariable.wordpress.com

AMITTRAS PAL is an amateur writer trying to make sense of the universe within in his own way, a little music, and a lot of jumbled words.
Blog: The Universe Within at www.vastnesswithin.wordpress.com
Instagram: @amittraspal

BRAEDEN MICHAELS is an American author and creator of Deconstructive Literature. He has been published in *Static Dreams volume 1: A Dark Anthology from Twisted Minds.* His debut poetry book *The Raven's Poison* is due summer 2020.
Blog: braedenmichaels.com
Instagram: @braedenmichaels

BRANDON WHITE is a poet, songwriter, proud husband and father of twins from Fort Smith, Arkansas. Brandon has released multiple EPs and albums (all available on your favorite streaming service) and will see his debut poetry collection, *The Year That Stole the Light Away,* in the summer of 2020.
Blog: www.brandonwhitemusicandpoetry.com
Instagram: @brandonwhitemusicandpoetry
Goodreads: www.goodreads.com/ brandonwhitemusicandpoetry

CANDICE LOUISA DAQUIN, French-American editor and writer, was lead editor of *SMITTEN,* a collection of love poetry by women for women, co-editor of *We Will Not Be Silenced,* an anthology of poetry inspired by the *#metoo* movement and is the author of five collections of her own poetry. Her work can be found in bookstores and online.
Blog: www.thefeatheredsleep.com
Instagram: @candicedaquin
Goodreads: www.goodreads.com/ Candice Louisa Daquin

CASSA BASSA is a China-born Australian poet who works with the poor and homeless in Australia which gives her a special insight into those that suffer. An inquisitive writer that was a bit of a misfit as a child, she has blossomed into her writing.
Blog: flickerofthoughts.com
Instagram: @cassa_bassa

CG TENPENNY is a writer of poetry and prose.
Blog: www.moltenpoetry.com

CHRIS NELSON was born in a small town in the east of England but grew up in Birmingham. After leaving school he studied computing at what was then Wolverhampton Polytechnic, before deciding that it was not a career path he wanted to follow. He retrained as a teacher and has taught in a primary school in Dudley since the mid-1980s. He lives in Stourbridge with his wife and two children.
Blog: chrisnelson61.wordpress.com

EMJE MCCARTY has been writing, drawing, and trying to figure out how to save the world for as long as she can remember and will continue to do so. She lives in the driftless region of Wisconsin with her four feral kids and a half-trained dog.
Blog: www.quixoticmama.com
Instagram: @quixoticmama

GARY BRADSHAW is a Bejing-based international school educator, poet, and writer who has written a few fine poems and a great many rubbishy ones.

HIDDEN BEAR is a Mechoopda poet and author originally from Northern California where his tribe is based but currently living in North Carolina. After self-publishing his book *Moleskine on a Coffee Table* he transitioned to writing on his blog about his experience reclaiming the culture of his tribe. Growing up without his traditional culture he has been using poetry to connect to the culture, art, and spirit of his people.
Blog: hiddenbear.home.blog
Instagram: @hiddenbearpoet

J MATTHEW WATERS was born in Rock Island, Illinois in 1961 and grew up across the Mississippi in Davenport, Iowa. He graduated from the University of Iowa in 1984 with a BA in English. You can find his work at Amazon, on his poetry blog, and on Twitter.
Blog: jdubqca.com
Instagram & Twitter: @jdubqca
Goodreads: www.goodreads.com/jdubqca

JAMILA WARDAK is a twice published poet and public relations student at California State University, Long Beach with a passion for beauty and poetry. Jamila is currently working on her own skincare line while managing her blog that focuses on beauty, poetry, and healing. Feel free to check out the sites or reach out to her on social media.
Blogs: jamilasbicycle.blog or jamilawardak.com
Instagram: @jamilasbicycle

JANET SAWATSKY is a writer and photographer living on the left coast of Canada.
Blog: womenofacertainagedotca.com

JESSE LEE STAGGS
Instagram: @white_stag_poetry

LAYNE AMBROSE is a lover of many things… but most of all music, writing, and family…
Blog: chewing-on-glass.com
Twitter: @Chew_On_Glass
Goodreads: www.goodreads.com/Ambrose

LEON JONES truly is a Living Canvas. If it's not writing poetry, songs, and inspirational messages, it is singing and dancing like nobody's watching. Art is in his blood. Born in New Jersey and currently residing in Michigan, Leon has also done public speaking for disability advocacy and is a recipient of the *Spirit of Detroit* award.
*Instagram: @Livingcanvas84_*

M ENNENBACH is a lot of things. Poet. Writer. Father. Fool. He writes from the heart and emotion that may be strange, raw, or disturbing. He is from Illinois but lives in Texas. His kids are the most important part of his life. His books *Notches* and *(un)poetic* can be found at any major book seller.
Blog: Mike's Manic Word Depot at mennenbach.com

MARK RYAN was born in Oxford, growing up in the shadow of the dreaming spires. He studied film at London Metropolitan University, graduating to M.A in Film Theory. His work leans, bends, and sways to the metaphysical and supernatural, with a tendency to dabble in the macabre.
Blog: havocandconsequences.wordpress.com
Twitter: @MarkRyan8289
Goodreads: www.goodreads.com/ loved13

MARK TULIN is a former family therapist who lives in Santa Barbara, California. A poetry publisher once likened his work to artist Edward Hopper on how he grasps unusual aspects of people and their lives. Mark has two poetry chapbooks: *Magical Yogis* and *Awkward Grace* available on Amazon. His upcoming book, *The Asthmatic Kid and Other Stories* will be published in August 2020.
Blog: www.crowonthewire.com
Instagram: @crowonthewire_poetry
Twitter: @Crow_writer

ODY WEST started painting to combat depression. He has created a whole new style of art known as *Rorschach Abstract.*
Instagram: @westody
Facebook: @odywestshow

PIANO GIRL is a wife, mom of three young adults, and an elementary music teacher. She is most at home when sitting at the piano. She enjoys writing honest, personal stories and reflections about life. Writing helps calm her sometimes over-thinking brain.
Blog: pianogirlthoughts.com
Instagram: @kmariemorris

REDCAT is a lifelong bookworm that thinks reading, writing poetry and prose, music and dance makes life worth living. She trained as a soloist, sang in several choirs, acted and danced all through childhood and adolescence. Originally from the deep woods, this fiery redhead now makes home in Stockholm, Sweden, where you might run into her dancing the night away in one of the city's techno-clubs.
Blog: redcat.wordpress.com

RIVER DIXON has unknowingly found himself trapped in the incessant heat and beauty of Arizona. It is here, along with his family, that he finds solace stringing together words in an attempt to find a structure or sequence that may one day makes sense of all this.
Blog: www.thestoriesinbetween.com
Twitter: @Potters_Grove

ROBERT BIRKHOFER is a dreamer and a coffee drinker. He lives in Arizona with his wife and their two cats. More of Robert's work is available to read on his website, The Mad Puppeteer.
Blog: The Mad Puppeteer at themadpuppeteer.com
Instagram: the_madpuppeteer

S J REIZLEIN lives in leafy Worcestershire, England. A fair amount of his time is spent reading, writing, traveling, and listening to music. He even finds time for exercise, on the odd occasion.

SHANE WINDHAM is a full-time author, songwriter, YouTuber, and game designer. Learn more at shanewindham.com.
Blog: wordfireprose.blogspot.com
Instagram: @wordfireprose
Goodreads: goodreads.com/shanewindham

STEVEN BRYSON is a hobby artist and passionate about improving mental health after suffering a breakdown some time ago. He lives on the Isle of Wight in the UK with his wife and daughter.
Blog: www.wordpress.com/smallislandthinker
Instagram: @smallislandscribbler

TJ is a Canadian blogger who primarily writes erotic musings, poetry, short stories, and dabbles in abstract art, using it as a vehicle for the exploration of her fetish with acrylic paint. She has been known to use various body parts as paintbrush, palette, and canvas. She talks to trees and wishes she had a pet snake…but will settle for a dog.
Blog: www.thelustfulempress.blog

TRISTAN DRUE ROGERS has had his writing and poetry featured in literary magazines (such as *Vamp Cat, Genre: Urban Art, Weird Mask,* and more) and horror anthologies (such as *100 Word Horrors Book 3* and *Twenty Twenty*). He is also a Site Contributor for *Genre: Urban Arts.* Tristan lives with his lovely wife Sarah and their son Rhett in Texas.
Blog: www.tristandrue.wordpress.com
Twitter: @RogersDrue

VALENTINA SALDAÑA is an author, actress, and artist from Texas. You can connect with her and experience more of her creations at her blog. She is currently working on her first book of speculative fiction short stories.
Blog: www.wordsmonstersme.wordpress.com

www.ingramcontent.com/pod-product-compliance
Lightning Source LLC
LaVergne TN
LVHW091003080826
845145LV00003B/1107

* 9 7 8 1 7 3 3 0 8 0 8 5 9 *